HEAD
HUNTERS

HEAD HUNTERS

ROBERT McKINNON, M.A.

SCOPE BOOKS LIMITED

First published April 1982

© Scope Books Ltd 1982
3 Sandford House, Kingsclere,
Newbury, Berkshire RG15 8PA

British Library Cataloguing in Publication Data

McKinnon, Robert
  The headhunters.
  1. Executives — Great Britain
  2. Recruiting of employees — Great Britain
  I . Title
  658.4'07   HF554.9

ISBN 0 906619 10 6

Cover design by AJF Studios, Thatcham
Typeset by Signland Limited, Farnham, Surrey
Printed and bound in Great Britain by
Billing and Sons Limited
Guildford, London, Oxford, Worcester

Contents

About the Author

After six years of remarkably ordinary service in the R.A.F., **Robert McKinnon** says that he somehow found the will power to return to Glasgow University where he took an arts degree in 1947.

Though failing to set the Thames on fire when he came to London, he nevertheless enjoyed the modest compensation of being appointed editor of *Personnel Management & Methods* (now *Personnel Management*) in 1953, and has been a business journalist ever since. He is also consultant editor to the Royal Society for the Prevention of Accidents and he points out that today "occupational safety and health has an ever growing business dimension."

Robert McKinnon is the author of innumerable articles on management and human relations for an improbable variety of publications and among others, is a regular contributor to *The Director* and *Chief Executive*, and is the author of one or two books on the subject, including what he describes as "a Code of Practice of tome-like proportions for the Institute of Employment Consultants — so in a sense *The Headhunters*, dealing as it does with the world of top jobs, takes me to a higher plateau in the same field."

As with any dyed-in-the-wool journalist, his leisure interests centre on his work and talking shop, though he admits he once had an eye for the ball. "Even that", he adds, "found its way into print through eight very happy years I spent as editor of *Sport & Recreation* and three as a soccer correspondent for *The Sunday Telegraph* in its formative years."

Author's Foreword

I hope this book can at least boast the negative virtue of not attempting to tell readers how to become rich and successful headhunters in six easy lessons. I doubt in fact if anyone, headhunters included, could do that. We know the job requires a mix of tenacity, ruthlessness, sensitivity and the ability to market oneself, but none of us can acquire such qualities merely by reading about them.

Rather, I have sought to describe the way in which headhunters go about their business, the problems they encounter, the service they claim to provide and how they see the future of the activity. I have also aired such controversial issues as "poaching", "value for money" and "contingency fees", and have let them speak for themselves as far as possible. At the same time, I have indulged an author's privilege by interspersing the material with views and prejudices of my own.

Oddly enough, there is not nearly as much information on headhunters and their activities as managers and businessmen may be disposed to think. There are plenty of case histories, but information on these, for obvious reasons, has to be cloaked in anonymity, and in any case many of these are repetitive in substance. Facts and figures on trends within the industry are hard to come by, however, and much of what I have quoted in these pages contains an element not so much of guesswork as of calculation.

The limited nature of the data reflects perhaps the secretiveness which pervades the industry.

That said, I must stress that, as a tribe, I did not find headhunters to be the grey, furtive men of current legend. On the contrary, they seemed to me like any other cross-section of managers, some flamboyant and extrovert, others quiet and restrained and others somewhat betwixt and between. In sum, I found them invariably helpful, though some of their answers were guarded or wrapped up in a company message, and I would like to thank here and now all those who so kindly gave me of their time, knowledge and opinions. I am most grateful to them.

This book contains no sexual material, scandalous or otherwise, but readers may find this a refreshing change. The reason is simply that, in this regard, headhunting seems to be a very moral profession; I did not come across as much as a hint of favours for jobs, and thus vanishes any hope of serialisation in *The News of the World*. Headhunting is also an almost exclusively masculine activity — carried out by males on behalf of males — though I did speak to one woman headhunter who thought that feminine sensitivity and intuition could and did make a valuable contribution to the profession.

I would round off these few remarks with the story of the judge who presided over a tax case in which F.E. Smith (later Lord Birkenhead) argued his client's cause with great skill and clarity, taking the whole court unerringly through the most complicated legal nuances. Suddenly the judge interrupted: "Mr Smith", he said, "I have been listening to you for nearly an hour and I am none the wiser." "Possibly not, my Lord", Smith replied, "but you are much better informed."

If this volume can achieve something of the latter, I will be quite satisfied.

Robert McKinnon, January 1982

1
Search or Selection

What's in a name?

The term "headhunter" is by no means one which is universally approved by recruitment consultants, many of whom still regard it as a crude and inaccurate description of their activities in much the same way that a psychiatrist may bridle at the use of "head shrinker" or a dentist at "ivory snatcher". We may live in a permissive society, but that does not imply that a sense of dignity — or, if one prefers it, stuffiness — has totally vanished from the professional scene.

Some recruitment specialists, on the other hand, accept the description quite cheerfully — perhaps they think it reflects an image of vigour and determination — while others maintain that, technically, they are not headhunters at all. These are usually selection consultants who argue that the term applies only to those in the search end of the industry. My own view is that the distinction is real but of scant importance. Both selection and search consultants provide a client service aimed at finding the best man (in most cases) or woman for a specific post, for which the job specification and the terms and conditions of employment are agreed in advance. It makes not the slightest difference in principle to the client whether the post is filled as a result of a dragnet operation based on judicious advertising or through a kind of private eye quest which concentrates on perhaps half a

1

dozen known individuals, though the client may prefer one type of operation to another for a variety of other reasons. One other point about the title of this book. Over the past twenty-five years since search and selection consultants have been operating on any scale in this country, they have been called many things — and not all of them flattering. "Flesh pedlars", "talent poachers", "body snatchers" are some of the sobriquets which spring to mind, and it seems to me that "headhunters" is no worse than any of these and every bit as apposite. Again, it is a term widely accepted in the recruitment industry itself and among those who have been the object of its attention. People who have been headhunted are invariably flattered by the fact, even if they were not finally appointed to the post in question. Hence the title of this book.

Which method?
More and more recruitment consultancies are in fact coming to use a mix of both search and selection in the course of their assignments, but it is worth looking very briefly at the key steps in each approach, bearing in mind that the method will vary in detail from consultancy to consultancy and from assignment to assignment. Basically, search is an upmarket type of operation concerned with finding people for top management jobs usually at director or chief executive level, though it is also used extensively to track down people for key posts in the technical or production control field — for instance, director of research or head of an oil exploration team. After the job specification has been agreed with the client, the search consultant is on his own with only his experience, imagination and perhaps but not always a few contacts to help him. At the same time he will be expected to come up with a short list of perhaps four or five names within an agreed time, and he may also be expected to help the client in making the final choice and in subsequently checking out the success or otherwise of that choice. For a number of reasons, confidentiality and anonymity are usually "twin pillars" of the process, so if the headhunter

elects to use advertisements, these will invariably appear under a box number and be so worded as to give away as little as possible about the identity of the client.

With the selection method, as stated, the dragnet of selective advertising is employed, though here again the identity of the client may not be made explicit in the early stages of the process. As a rule, selection is used more widely in the case of middle and junior management vacancies, or in the case of senior posts — such as chief accountant — where the requirement is not too esoteric. If asked why firms and other organisations should use his services instead of going through their own personnel departments, the selection consultant can put forward a number of arguments. These include:

i.   access to extensive knowledge of the market concerned;

ii.   wide experience in managerial job analysis and design, in drawing up recruitment advertisements, in interviewing assessment and in terms and conditions of employment.

iii.   a considerable saving in company senior management time; only candidates with qualifications relevant to the post in question are seen.

It may of course be argued also that an efficient personnel department should have the necessary skills to carry out the above functions itself, but it is also true that many such departments are today bogged down in the quagmire of human and industrial relations and wage and salary negotiation. There is a good deal of evidence to support this assertion. In my own case, for instance, I attended some three years ago the annual conference of the Institute of Personnel Management at Harrogate for the first time since 1958, and was amazed at the radical change in the whole nature and atmosphere of the event. Apart from a discernible swing to the Left among the speakers and the content of their contributions, a flourishing exhibition of what I can describe only as the hardware of personnel management had been added to the conference, in the shape of pension schemes, publications, wages payment systems and of course have led to better human and industrial relations, but it industrial catering services and the like. All this may not have led to better human and industrial relations, but it has certainly eaten into the time personnel departments can spare for other activities.

To return, however, to the selection process. The five-star approach, so to speak, will involve as a first step a visit by the consultant to the client's premises, during which the consultant should gain a better understanding of the client's needs and of the "chemistry" of his organisation, thus enabling him to make an accurate assessment of the post to be filled, and of the type of candidate to look for and the terms of employment. The consultant will then submit for client approval a recommendation on detailed costs, including the cost of advertising and a draft advertisement for the post. If approved, the advertisement is placed in a selected publication (usually one of the "quality" newspapers) after which the consultant evaluates the applications and interviews and assesses candidates vis-a-vis the job specification. He will then present the client with a short list of recommended candidates, and keep himself informed of progress throughout the assignment until an appointment has been made. Finally, about twelve months later, the consultant will contact the client again to discuss the performance of the person appointed.

Such, as stated, is the five-star approach, but selection can be a much more primitive affair, in which there is no visit to the client's premises, nor much agonising over the advertisement design or substance, nor indeed any follow-up after the appointment. Even preparation of a short list can be a hurried, skimped operation (sometimes because of client pressure) during which the consultant may "salt" the candidate list with names from his own files.

Of course, as in any other field, people pay for what they get. I have been told of consultancies, operating in specific industries such as catering or transport, which charge as little as 5% of annual salary for their services in making a placement. In the five-star bracket, however, consultancy fees for a single assignment will generally total 20% of the initial annual remuneration of the successful candidate (plus of course the cost of advertisements). Fees are often presented at different stages of the assignment: for example, 5% of annual salary when the client authorises the assignment; 10% when the shortlist is submitted, and 5% when the successful candidate accepts the job. The consultant will also charge the client for any necessary travel and subsistence expenses.

Comparative costs

An executive search assignment is usually thought of in management circles as being more expensive than a selection assignment, but this may no longer be true of today bearing in mind the rocketing cost of advertising, especially in "quality" newspapers such as *The Daily Telegraph, The Financial Times* or *The Sunday Times*, which for various reasons are three "favourites" of the selection men. Sometimes, in fact, the cost of selection can be higher than that of search.

"There's a point at which we pitch our minimum fee", explained Garry Long, group managing director of M.S.L. International Management Consultants, one of the pioneer headhunting firms in Britain, "perhaps at £5,000 or £6,000. At this figure you can't "search" a chief accountant at £15,000 a year – he's got to be found through selection – but a chief animal feedstuffs chemist at the same salary is a different story. But it's often cheaper to search at 30% of a £15,000 salary than to do the job through selection where we would charge 20% of salary plus the cost of advertisements."

M.S.L. it should be added, handles all levels of executive appointments but tends to specialise functionally in middle management jobs, claiming at the same time to design a service for most slots in the market.

"Don't believe that a search consultant never advertises", Garry Long added. "They often insert "blind ads" under a box number. Equally, it's not true that good people do not reply to advertisements. Indeed, I think I could fill any senior job through advertisements as well as through search."

However, the prevailing view in the headhunting industry as a whole is that the higher the post, the more likely it is that the search method will be used, so it follows that the the consultancy operating exclusively in the search field is likely to find itself more upmarket than the selection firm operating over a wider spectrum. Even so, much of what Garry Long told me was supported by Peter Prentice, managing partner of Tyzack & Partners Ltd, another internationally known recruitment consultancy based on London.

"There's no doubt whatever", he commented, "that selection nowadays can be every bit as expensive as search. With a 17cm triple column advertisement in *The Sunday Times* costing about £2,000, the overall cost of advertising at what may be termed "the lower end of the market" can in fact exceed the consultancy fee. On the other hand, some jobs are not identifiable by normal search techniques, which must have been the reason why the American search firm, Russell Renolds, took a full page in *The Economist* early in 1981 to draw the attention of executives all over the world to a top job in the Far East. Or, again, top appointments in the public sector often have to be advertised under policy rules, as was the case with the job of personnel director at the B.B.C. Very often, in fact, I think search consultants would like to combine the two approaches even though the terms of the assignment rule it out."

A third view was put forward by David Blamey of Spencer Stuart Management Consultants London, part of an international group which, like one or two others, claim to have pioneered search techniques in the United Kingdom. It is not the purpose of this book to examine and assess such claims — no doubt most of those concerned could produce solid evidence — but that the claims are made at all reflects the growing awareness among the headhunters that their activities are now "hallowed" by time and accepted by commerce and industry. Anyhow David Blamey made the point that "the way in which we recruit depends on the circumstances. An advertisement, for example, is unlikely to attract a top executive in a highly yechnical field, but it is highly effective where the market is wide, and so we use advertisements even though we are pioneers of search techniques. What's more, because search has become more "respectable" it is becoming more and more acceptable to use both methods and at the same time. Nor is it true that good and busy people do not read advertisements."

Blamey went on to say that Spencer Stuart was specially interested in spreading an understanding of executive search and had been developing the technique as a means of finding non-executive directors for the boards of various British companies, "an area", he claimed, "in which many British businesses are weak." For its part, Tyzack & Partners runs a similar scheme in conjunction with the Institute of Directors. It is all part of the expanding use of search/selection, which is looked at later.

A precision tool

Executive search, then, is a high precision instrument and, as such, should be used with discrimination. It is a truth expressed in a different and dramatic way by John Reid, managing director of Executive Search Ltd. "It's true that search can be applied at any level", he agreed, "and if you want the best tea lady in London I can get her for you, but she'd be tremendously expensive. At salaries of over £16,000 a year, however, search tends to be the better proposition."

A basic weakness of the search approach, however, especially where a consultancy tends to specialise in a given industry or activity — for example, finance, computing, publishing, chemicals, transport and so on, is that an incestuous situation can emerge, one in which the recruiter gets to know everyone worth knowing and rarely comes in contact with new blood. The problem is aggravated by the very tight specifications laid down by the client looking for someone to fill a top job, so the search man not infrequently finds himself operating in a market consisting of perhaps only six individuals, none of whom may wish to move. In such a situation, inevitably, the temptation to rob Peter to pay Paul can be very strong, and this is why most reputable search firms operate to a strict code of not poaching from their own clients — or at least of waiting perhaps a couple of years before doing so!

The selection firm, by contrast, through the advertising trawl, does attract fresh blood, though mostly at junior and middle management levels; still, the man of tomorrow ought to be spotted as soon as possible in their careers. This fact has created an additional facility within the professional recruitment industry — namely, the agency file or, more cynically, "the old boy network in which the same names are shuffled and keep re-appearing". A properly run agency register does, nevertheless, serve as a means of giving a second and third chance to able people who may have been passed over through no fault of their own, a state of affairs which applies in particular among executives with a technical or scientific background. "I regard our agency side", said Mike Gernat, head of Electronic Computer & Management Appointments Ltd, a business based at Royston, Herts, "as a very valuable third limb to our business."

Search and selection, then, do differ radically in approach, but it is a difference which need not be laboured too much, for each can be regarded primarily as a feature of the overall headhunting operation. In the next chapter, the place of headhunting is looked at vis-a-vis the whole pattern of executive recruitment.

2

The State of the Art

An ever-improving image

"Whether the CBI could or would have secured Sir Terence Beckett without headhunters Spencer Stuart or British Steel Ian McGregor without Russell Reynolds is a moot point. The fact is that, whereas for years members of the shadowy profession of search consultancy were only ever referred to in specialist personnel and recruitment circles, now not only their existence but even their names are being bandied about like pop stars."

This comment from the November 1980 edition of *Personnel Management* may err towards exaggeration but it contains a grain of truth. Headhunters have come a long way since the 1950s when very little was known of their activities among industry and commerce at large, while that which *was* known was all too often seen through a distorting lens. Managements, on the whole, were highly suspicious: headhunters were seen either as skilful manipulators of an old boy network collecting fat fees for doing very little or as a species of witchdoctor purporting to be able to tell whether a candidate was any good "the moment he walks through the door."

All this has largely changed or is changing. True, quite a number of firms still regard search consultants as people who charge substantial fees for minimal effort, while quite a number of personnel departments (notably in the United

9

Kingdom) view them as interlopers — an attitude directed at selection as well as search firms. In general, however, with each year that passes, the recruitment consultant is becoming more and more "accepted" even where he is still regarded as a kind of "necessary evil". On both sides of the Atlantic there is strong evidence of a steady growth in headhunting, and this has continued despite the recession of recent years. This is not just the considered opinion of the headhunters themselves, who nevertheless are right when they point out that the demand for top executive talent becomes keener than ever when business survival is at stake.

"I think there is very little doubt (although I have not carried out a substantial analysis) that the demand for the services of executive search consultants, has grown in recent years."

This is the view of R.A.B. Gowlland, managing partner of Egon Zehnder International, a consultancy with branches in 18 major cities of the world. He stresses, however, that it is doubtful whether it has grown as rapidly in these recent years of recession. "What has undoubtedly happened", he claims, "is that more and more of the "business" has been chanelled to the more professional firms and the more international firms", adding that the more professional consultancies are usually the more international.

Gowlland quotes another reason for the growth in demand — namely, the increasing "respectability" of executive search.

"In the early days", he says, "executive search was somewhat looked down upon, and this attitude was fostered by the advertising recruitment firms. Nowadays executive search is considered the best way of solving top management problems and few people have any hesitation in asking the leading professional executive search firms to carry out searches on their behalf. It seems likely therefore that demand will continue to grow during the 1980s, although perhaps at a slower rate."

Nigel Rugman, a director of Management Appointments Ltd, takes a similar view of the headhunter market, but claims that "it is also true to say that the field is becoming increasingly competitive and search consultancies are being asked to "pitch" for assignments versus other appointments.

"Companies", he explained, "are coming to realise that they've got a choice, so they will telephone a search consultancy and ask: 'let's hear what you've got to say'. This type of preliminary enquiry is on the increase, but on the other hand the headhunting profession is no longer in an age when we have to prove we've got something to offer."

A third view came from George H.G. Harris of Canny Bowen & Associates Ltd, another leading international firm of headhunters. "The activity continues to grow", he said, "because there is very little "natural wastage" at the highest levels of management, besides which in hard times firms must take a hard look at the management team, though it's different in the frills of management such as planning and communication."

Eurosurvey Ltd, another well established search consultancy with branches in five countries — United Kingdom, Belgium, Holland, France and West Germany, reinforces George Harris' comment on the "frills" of management. In a special report, *Management Trends in 1980*, based on client and candidate interviews, it stresses that "the vast majority of our assignments for industry are for line management. There is but little demand for appointments which are aimed at bringing intellectual contributions to the company. Staff appointments — such as corporate planning — are very much at a discount and are considered as a luxury."

"Service industries, for example, banking, insurance, leisure and consulting", the report goes on, "continue to maintain a high demand for management, and there is also a growing demand for professional management from non-profit organisations such as pension funds, social foundations, semi-government bodies, educational organisations and even from government itself."

"As for the executive search profession, we are happy to observe an ever growing appreciation for its role and the help which it can give managements, provided it meets the increasingly high standards both in terms of pure ethics and actual results. Very rightly, both clients and candidates are becoming increasingly critical and this is an attitude which we very much welcome as it can only serve to improve standards and add to the reputation of what is still a relatively young profession."

Fun with figures

Such figures as there are — and most must be described as "guesstimates" — confirm that the search industry has been growing steadily in recent years. A prime source, as far as the United Kingdom and Western Europe is concerned, were the findings of a special survey conducted in 1979 by the Geneva-based partnership, Consultex SA, covering 100 search firms operating from 160 offices in Belgium, France, the Netherlands, Switzerland, U.K. and West Germany. Headhunting the survey underlined, is most developed in France, the United Kingdom and West Germany (though, technically, it is illegal in the Federal Republic, so consultants serving that market operate from outside its borders) which are served by an estimated 111 search firms carrying out approximately 5,000 assignments per year. In 1979, these firms earned a total fee revenue (in terms of U.S. dollars) of $70 million, but the full basic details are given in the table below:

The Western European Search and Recruitment Markets in 1979

Country	Fee income ($ million)	Number of assignments	Number of firms	Number of known consults
UK	25	2,000	40	162
West Germany	25	2,000	35	105
France	20	1,200	36	141
Belgium	14	650	22	48
Switzerland	13	600	24	60
Netherlands	5	260	13	26
Total	102	6,710	170	542

Two points should be noted right away about the figures in the above table. First, although providing an adequate bird's eye view of the size of the search industry, they are three years old, and more headhunting firms have emerged since in this area of the world. Again, the figures do not include details of consultancies engaged in selection based upon recruitment advertising — which, indeed, is thought to generate a much greater fee income than straightforward search.

Nevertheless, the figures do underline that executive search is one of the most lucrative and fastest growing sectors of management consulting in Western Europe. Fees, to put it modestly, are high; a typical search assignment, according to the Consultex survey, will cost at least $15,000 and could run to hundreds of thousands of dollars in some cases, with fees based on 30% to 40% of the annual starting salary of the chosen candidate (In the United Kingdom, most of the leading search firms charge 25% to 30% of starting salary, though more and more headhunters are now charging straight fees plus expenses based on their assessment of the complexity of an assignment and the time it is likely to require for successful completion.)

Further light on the British scene was cast by A.E. Young, chairman of Alexander Hughes & Associates (U.K.) Ltd, who (talking to me in the spring of 1981) estimated total fee income for the U.K. executive search market at £5½ million. This is about half the total quoted for the U.K. in the Consultex survey but, according to Young, "it is produced by 110 search consultants in the field, and a very competent search man will produce about £60,000 to £70,000 a year, though the average is about £50,000 a year." Again, for its part, Consultex quoted a figure of 162 known consultants for the British market, whereas Young's total is only about two-thirds of this.

Two further "guesstimates" were supplied by George Harris of Canny Bowen and Garry Long of Management Selection Ltd. Harris quoted an annual turnover of £6 to £8 million for executive search only, while Long put annual

U.K. turnover in what he calls the "jobs industry" — namely, search plus selection "where a third party is involved" — at £12 to £15 million a year.

Few if any of the sums quoted can of course be regarded as gospel if only because opinions vary widely on what constitutes search as distinct from selection. However, if we settle for the Consultex 1979 estimate of $102 million as the total executive search fee income for Western Europe, it expresses more dramatically than any words the degree of acceptance the activity has won for itself — and this despite the fact that, according to the Consultex findings, only 70% of all headhunting findings result in a candidate's being appointed. On the other hand, if the placement rate reached 100%, there would indeed be cause for suspicion.

A pointer to the lack of statistical information about recruitment consultancies emerges from the fact that it was not until the autumn of 1980 that any directory of United Kingdom firms working in this field was published. This appeared under the title of *The Executive Grapevine* by Robert B. Baird (by Executive Grapevine Publications Ltd of Blackheath, London) and it gives details of some 175 search and selection consultancies operating up and down the country — but the vast majority based in London — classified by function, industry, salary range and location. Some of the information it contains is disputed by the search and selection industry itself — notably details concerning the size and number of assignments handled by individual consultancies, for the industry is certainly not without its petty jealousies — nevertheless *The Executive Grapevine* has filled a gap in the management literature market. It also underlines how this sector of consulting has grown in recent years, even though the author has done his best to include only the highly reputable firms.

Anyhow, in an introduction to *The Executive Grapevine*, Mike Dixon of *The Financial Times* noted that over the years many managers and specialists had complained to him about the lack of information on recruitment consultancies in the United Kingdom and of having no means of identifying appropriate consultancies. "Others", he added, "were members of the sadly increasing army of jobless executives, keen to go beyond applying for such likely looking jobs as turned up in the advertisements and to lay their career records before consultants likely to have need of them."

Laudable as the latter service may be, it should be emphasised that very few search or selection firms undertake the counselling of redundant executives — there are one or two specialist consultancies doing this type of work — and those who do so usually undertake this job as a special favour to a valued client. It is an activity as yet far more highly developed in the U.S.A., where by common consent the whole executive recruitment industry tends to set the pace and throw up many of the ideas for the rest of the Western world.

The American scene

Here again there are no precise figures as to the total number of firms operating in the American recruitment market nor indeed as to annual fee turnover, but a reasonable estimate is that this has now reached $250 million while, according to the Association of Executive Recruiting Consultants, there are some consultancies in the country as a whole; more than 150 search firms are listed in New York City alone.

In general, the search market in the U.S.A. is regarded as being much more "saturated" than is the case in Britain and Western Europe, with the result that developments taking place these days on the other side of the Atlantic tend to take the form of refinements, such as new specialisms or approaches to recruiting, rather than of straightforward growth. According to Roger M. Kenny, a partner and senior vice president of Spencer Stuart & Associates, executive search activities have flourished in America "because of the phenomenal growth of our gross national product since 1950, a growth which outpaced industry's ability to develop top management."

"In this period", he added, "there also has been a growing

acceptance by corporations that they can't, and probably shouldn't, "home grow" all their own executives."

Another stimulus to the expansion of executive search has been the increase in the international operations of many American businesses. Indeed, according to A.E. Young of Alexander Hughes & Associates, "about one-third of the assignments passing through the London end of the market originate in North America. The international market could in fact double within the next five years."

As stated, with saturation has come refinement — by function as well as by industry. The American Management Associations lists five distinct types of activity, or service, one or more of which is offered by the headhunting industry in the U.S.A. These are described briefly below:

1. **Executive Search.** These organisations work for the employer looking for an executive to fill a specific position. They are paid by the employer for making the search and for out-of-pocket expenses of advertising, telephone, travel or testing but do not charge the individual executive who may be placed with the client company.
   (This of course is very much the same as executive search as understood in this country.)

2. **Executive Job Counselling.** These firms work directly for the individual executive. Through counselling sessions (and perhaps with the aid of psychological tests) they help the executive to assess his strengths, identify types of job in line with his experience, abilities and interests, and/or map out a career plan or job-finding strategy. The executive pays the fee, which applies whether he secures a position or not.
   (Consultancies like these are not unknown in the United Kingdom, but are still very much in their infancy over here.)

3. **Executive Marketing.** These organisations actively help

the individual to attract the attention of employers. They may assist him in preparing a resumé (a *curriculum vitae*), compile a mailing list of possible employers, and/or send out a quantity of letters and resumés suggesting him to employers. The executive pays the fee, which applies whether he secures a position or not.

4. **Licensed Personnel Agency.** These serve as intermediaries between employers and job seekers. They interview executives interested in new positions, evaluate their abilities and classify them according to job specification. Employers contact these agencies when they have openings, and the agency recommends suitable candidates for interview. The fee is commonly paid by the individual executive but applies only if he eventually accepts a position with a company to which he has been referred. Some agencies refer candidates only to companies which agree to pay the fee.

5. **Job Register.** This type of service is essentially that of a clearing house or data bank through which details of the track records of individual executives are channelled to interested employers. When an employer advises the job register of a specific opening, their retrieval system locates the relevant resumes which are then forwarded to the employer. A register charges the individual executive a fixed amount for entering his resumé in the data bank, and the fee applies whether or not he secures a position.

It may of course be argued that similar services can be found in the executive recruitment industry on this side of the Atlantic. Many search and selection consultancies do keep extensive records — some computerised, some manual — which are in effect "registers" or "data banks", and this applies especially to consultancies working in a specific field such as computing, transport or P.R. and advertising. It is very doubtful, however, whether services of this kind have been developed over here to the same level of sophistication as in North America.

Nor is the "acceptability" of the headhunter any longer a problem in American industry and commerce. "In the U.S.A.", observed John Reid of Executive Search Ltd, "the chiefs of personnel departments retain and brief headhunters on their needs and actively cooperate with them in every way, as indeed they are expected to." It is a point also borne out by Roger Kenny of Spencer Stuart, who wrote some three years ago: "Even some of the major *Fortune 500* firms that have invested heavily in their own recruiting resources need occasional confidential surveys and discreet approaches to members of competition. Today, an executive search firm is perceived as an extension of a client's internal resources and both work hand-in-hand to achieve specific manpower goals."

Headhunting in perspective

Evidence which shows the headhunting industry in a buoyant condition must nevertheless also be seen in perspective. The fact is that the vast majority of executive placements in industry and elsewhere are still made through means other than search or selection — for example, through promotion from within, direct advertising, personal recommendations or even through the old boy network (where such a phenomenon exists). What is more, despite the rise of the headhunter, this basic state of affairs does not seem to have altered much over the past ten years.

All this is amply borne out in a joint survey carried out in 1980 by the British Institute of Management (B.I.M.) and the Institute of Personnel Management (I.P.M.) and published under the title of *Selecting Managers — How British Industry Recruits*. It is looked at here in some detail because of its importance and inherent interest. The survey results were based upon the answers given by 335 companies (representing a very healthy 28% response) within the manufacturing and services sectors but not the public sector, and four management categories were covered:

18

Senior manager: executives responsible for a major function and reporting to a member of the board;

Middle manager: executives responsible directly to senior management;

Junior manager: level of responsibility above first-line supervisor;

Specialist: personnel working in a staff or advisory capacity — for example, a legal adviser or work study officer.

Topics covered by the survey included such questions as who is involved in the various stages of recruitment and selection, sources of recruitment and selection and the extent of their use, attitudes towards these sources and the average time taken to fill a vacancy. Other sections looked at the contents of typical job advertisements, the interview, different selection methods, the qualities looked for when assessing candidates and the direct costs of recruitment.

The main conclusion emerging from this most useful exercise was that more than 75% of the sample used internal sources to recruit executives, and there is no reason to suppose that this figure does not reflect the general position as well. As to external sources of recruitment, the research findings indicated that the most widely used method is local press advertising, although its use dwindles as the size of the company increases; one could also add truthfully that the use of local press advertising diminishes as the level of appointment goes up — it is unlikely, for example, that a company would seek a chief executive through the pages of a parish pump publication. The survey also notes that "the higher up the management hierarchy one goes the less 'open' the recruitment method". Thus, although advertising is used widely when recruiting junior and middle managers, "appointments at more senior levels tend to be made on the basis of some form of internal assessment and/or personal contact".

For all that, the survey findings showed that only 14%
of companies make much use of management selection
consultants, a figure which plummets to 4% in the case of
executive search. The Government executive recruitment
agency, PER (of which more in a later chapter), is not
widely used either, according to the findings, with only
23% of companies using it occasionally. Of all external
sources of recruitment, respondents to the survey rated
the national press as the most effective and professional
registers as the least effective. Over half the companies
expressed themselves dissatisfied with the executive search
approach, though the survey does not make clear what
proportion of these companies had actually tried this method
of recruitment.

Baldly presented, the BIM/IPM survey findings can hardly
be said to fly the flag for the headhunting profession, so
these are worth examining more closely. The report itself
concedes that the figure of 4% for the number of respondents
using executive search consultancies regularly "is perhaps
hardly surprising since executive search is typically
used to fill "top level" or "one off" posts rather than for
normal recruitment exercises". It also noted a concentration
of use in London and the South East (where most British
headhunters are in fact located) and that the extent of use
increases with company size. "Even so", the report added,
"only 20% of companies with over 1,000 employees reported
anything more than a very occasional use of executive
search consultants."

The report's comments on the use of management selection consultants are even more intriguing. Whilst only 14%
of all respondents said that they made a lot of use of these
consultancies, the ratio increases to one in four in the case
of companies with more than 1,000 employees. "There is
a higher than average use in the London area", the report
claims, "reflecting both the location of the majority of
selection consultants and the fact that responsibility for
senior posts is frequently held at a head office location
which for many companies is based on London. This fact

is supported by the finding that 17% of companies which are part of a group make a lot of use of consultants compared with just 8% of those which are not part of a larger organisation."

The survey's comments on the headhunting profession cannot, however, be left at this point of comfortable compromise, because those firms taking part also voiced a number of criticisms and complaints against the tribe, which, it has to be admitted, are still commonly heard in commerce and industry. Management selection consultants, for instance, were rated highly in terms of being able to present suitable applicants, but only 6% of participating companies gave them any marks for cost effectiveness. The main criticism against them was that they are expensive, and they were also accused of failing to familiarise themselves sufficiently with the needs of their clients, of being "commission motivated" and of frequently ignoring the job specification in order to get one of their own candidates selected so that they could get their commission. Other respondents stated quite simply that "anyone who comes between us and the candidate is not welcome", while others thought that, in preparing shortlists, selection consultants always run the risk of throwing the baby out with the bathwater. That, however, is always a danger no matter who does the selecting, or how. On the other hand, the confidentiality inherent in the selection consultant's approach seemed to be recognised and valued.

This, likewise, was seen as the main advantage in using the services of an executive search man, especially when it is borne in mind that this is a method often favoured for top level recruitment. As with selection consultants, search specialists were also rated highly for presenting highly suitable applicants, but they were rated lowest in terms of cost effectiveness. This, it must be noted, is a complaint which has persisted since the earliest days of headhunting. I well remember myself a case in 1961 when a firm in the South-East of England making telecommunications equipment paid a headhunting firm the then enormous sum of £2,500

21

for finding an engineering director. The man selected was fired some six months later, but the sense of bitterness at the expense of it all lingered much longer.

But to return to the BIM/IPM report. A number of firms interviewed also expressed reservations about executive search methods and ethics. Most of these centred on the (by now, hackneyed) fear that headhunters will poach men even from their own clients, including even executives whom they have personally found and within six months to a year of the appointment having been made. Another comment was that "we don't like their ethics but it's sometimes necessary to use them", while one respondent alleged that "you run the risk with executive search of giving them access to the whole of your structure — this can be dangerous."

Criticisms of headhunters such as those in the survey findings are, as stated, still widely heard in commerce and industry, and are often justified, but this is an aspect of executive recruitment which is dealt with later. Here, however, it is only fair to add that headhunters can and do make entirely justifiable complaints against clients who all too often want the best as quickly and cheaply as possible while quoting minimal salary and employment perks for the successful candidate. If ever a condition of genuine give and take was essential, it should be found in the client-headhunter symbiosis.

One survey finding which should also be mentioned here has to do with the question of, Who does the selecting? The survey found that in 60% of respondent firms no single individual has overall responsibility for recruitment, though the person most likely to exercise this responsibility is the head of personnel, followed by the managing director of the firm. "However", the report adds, "as the selection process moves towards the final stages, there is a marked increase in the involvement of the line manager." In over half the companies interviewed, he it was who made the final decision on the appointment of junior and middle managers. In the case of senior management, as one would expect, the survey found that the final selection is usually made by the managing director or other board member, while at all levels of management the role of the personnel department was "markedly less prominent" at this stage. Headhunters themselves invariably report direct to the chief executive or to a panel of board members.

"After all", commented Peter Prentice, managing partner of Tyzack & Partners, "this is how it must be. You couldn't possibly have a situation in which the head of personnel was responsible for picking his own boss."

Where a head of personnel could be most useful in the matter of top-level appointments is in briefing the external recruitment consultant on company style and needs, on opportunities for advancement open to the newcomer and on the personal "chemistry" most acceptable to his employer's management team. After all, it is in the interests of everyone that the client gets good value for money. It cannot be said that cooperation of this kind is a marked feature of British industry, but it is a consummation devoutly to be wished, nevertheless.

This chapter has sought to collect together such statistical straws in the wind as are available in an attempt to give the reader some idea of the progress achieved by the headhunting business over the past 25 years. If we include the considerable amount of placements of executive talent in other areas of the world such as Africa, the Middle and Far East — areas of particular interest to British headhunters, incidentally — then it may not be wildly wrong to suggest that, world-wide, the executive recruitment industry is now enjoying an annual turnover in the region of 500 million U.S. dollars. The figure may be high, but the ability to manage a business successfully is a very scarce commodity.

Other straws in the wind

Yet money is by no means the only criterion of progress in this field. As we have seen, headhunters are by no means immune from criticism, and even downright hostility, but it cannot be denied that their number has multiplied simply because a need for them has been shown to exist. Again the industry itself has become much more self-confident and sophisticated — hence more efficient — not only as regards market knowledge and the drawing up of job specifications in consultation with clients but also in subtlety of approach as far as candidates are concerned.

Of course, as Roger Kenny points out, no two executive search firms are identical. Each consultancy stresses something that is special about itself, including multi-national networks, fee structure, research facilities, pre-search surveys, or executive orientation exercises. In Britain, I have found that several consultancies take much pride in having been "first in the field"; others make considerable play of their computer records and search capability, while one or two headhunters dismiss any kind of candidate records as a waste of time, claiming that market needs are changing all the time and that no two jobs are exactly the same and that, in any case, personnel files date very quickly. An opposite point of view is put forward by Anthony Langdon, a director of Eurosurvey Ltd: "Our whole operation is based upon massive research", he said, "and we will contact by telephone anything between 100 and 300 people during a typical assignment. The most difficult part of the job is to set up our initial research in order to target in on the right men. After that, the rest usually falls into place."

Other developments reflecting the growing power and prestige of the headhunter include the increasing use being made of his services by government agencies and semi-official organisations or, again, by firms large and small looking for the right type of non-executive director. It can be seen too in the steady development of specialist recruitment consultancies serving specific industries, one example being computing and micro-engineering where the demand may often be not for a managerial track record but for technical talent and experience, notably in the application of technology.

Speculation on the future of headhunting is left to the final chapter. Suffice it to say at this stage that we may well see all the developments already discussed expand and flourish over the next decade.

3
The Man and his Job

Still a male preserve

In this chapter I propose to let a number of leading British headhunters do a lot of the talking, about themselves and their jobs, but as a starting point let us consider the profile of the "typical" European search consultant put forward by Consultex SA of Geneva in its 1980 survey. In this document our consultant is described as "forty-two years old, male (99 per cent), has a college education and an advanced degree (often from a business school) and usually at least five years of industrial or business experience." As for the typical search firm, this is defined as small, with no more than five consultants (three or four in U.K. firms) operating from the same office.

Exceptions to these two thumbnail sketches will be found at every street corner, so to speak, but they are broadly accurate. I met only one woman headhunter director while interviewing for this book — Peggy Wingardh of Lyon & Brandfield Recruitment Ltd, a London partnership specialising in the P.R. and advertising field — though no doubt there are several others. Anyhow, Mrs Wingardh made the happy observation that "the very job of headhunting is a form of P.R." and went on to express the view that "all headhunters must have tact and the patience to listen, and this is what can sometimes make a woman better at the job than a man."

Be that as it may, headhunting is an overwhelmingly male activity at present, and Consultex is also right in stressing that most executive search men can boast a track record in commercial or industrial management, or in consulting, to which many can add the academic qualification of a degree in science or the arts. As to age, I have talked to headhunters in their middle sixties and early thirties though I am inclined to agree with Roger Stacey of Astron Appointments Ltd (a consultancy specialising in recruiting for the publishing industry) who thinks that maturity and experience of life are essential for the job and who most emphatically "does not believe in twenty-six-year-old headhunters." This, with one or two exceptions, is the consensus view. As Peter Prentice of Tyzack & Partners points out, "it would be absurd if a candidate for the post of chief executive in a well known company was to be interviewed by some inexperienced youngster just out of college, no matter how brilliant."

In physical appearance and personality, there is nothing to distinguish headhunters from any other group of executives. They come in all shapes and sizes, and none whom I have met looks or talks like Sherlock Holmes or Billy Graham. Most of them are well but quietly dressed, wear their hair reasonably short and are unfailingly courteous — even where there is a half-hearted attempt to cultivate a "rough diamond" image, such as one often finds among men and women in public relations. Most of them claim that sensitivity to the "chemistry" of a client or a candidate is a *sine qua non* of the job, and I have no reason to believe that the majority of them do not possess this attribute.

What did intrigue me during my researches for this book, however, was that the executive search and recruitment industry seems to be burdened with an inordinate share of backbiting, suspicions and petty jealousies. Members of the profession freely accuse others in the same field of not being "true headhunters", or of being "too big to do a proper job" or being "essentially selection people", while among the older established firms there is a tendency to claim the distinction of having been first in the field and of implying that rival firms are so many Johnnies-come-lately. This aspect of the recruitment industry is simply petty and unnecessary, and it is surprising that it should be so wide-spread among men of experience — and achievement — who purport to be skilled in spotting talent for others. The only explanation I can think of is that headhunting in its various forms, although increasingly accepted these days, is still not the confident, self-assured activity it would like to be.

Many of the leading consultancies, it must be added, are quite free of these symptoms of insecurity, and take the view that a competitor's success is good for the industry as a whole in the long run — and of course they are quite right.

Hard but rewarding

Again, the popular image of the headhunter as someone who sits in a plush office in the West End of London collecting substantial fees for a couple of telephone calls and a morning's interviewing is of course wildly exaggerated. Executive search consultancies do tend to congregate in the West End of London, and their offices are as a rule comfortable, not to mention elegant; this, however, is part of their shop window, and in any case London is often the location of the head offices of their clients. One can also state without fear of contradiction that most head-hunters make a good living and some achieve affluence even by today's standards. The job, moreover, is interesting: it involves travel, meeting people and the regular use of a wide range of skills. So there is no need to reach for a pocket handkerchief when considering the condition of the professional recruiter.

On the other hand, it must be added that the headhunter's job is not easy. It involves long, unsocial hours, including last-minute changes of schedule in order to have dinner (or, as often as not, breakfast) with a client or candidate, and there is the tedium of telephoning a targeted executive at his home in the evening in order to keep an assignment completely confidential. There is also often a struggle to persuade the client to alter the job specification or improve the salary and perks of the vacancy in question, and there can be the grisly problem of having to discourage a number of executives whose interest the headhunter has aroused in the first place.

"One becomes quite practised at this kind of thing", I was told by one well known executive search man with a base in the W.1 area. "The drill is to talk around the job at the initial meeting, keeping the approach as indirect and informal as possible, perhaps even asking the person you're speaking with if he knows of anyone who may be interested."

Another outright chore of the job, especially in the case of the selection consultant, is the sheer amount of costly and time consuming red tape. A job advertisement may attract anything from 100 to 500 replies, all of which have to be read and processed, even if only a courteous rejection is involved. Even setting up interviews can turn into a major headache, involving the by no means inconsiderable problem of arranging mutually convenient times and dates.

That, however, is part and parcel of the job, very much as traffic jams and third-rate hotels are part of the lot of most sales reps. What is more, there are times — and every honest headhunter will admit it — when assignments are successfully completed in a matter of days rather than weeks or months.

For example, Peter Chalkley, managing director of Sabre International Search, tells of one assignment handled by his firm on behalf of an electronics conglomerate, a multinational, seeking a managing director for its British subsidiary. The Big White Chief was due to come over from the U.S.A. in seven days' time, and he wanted to interview a short-list of six during his visit.

"The seven days included a bank holiday", Peter Chalkley added, "but through a process of frantic research and knowledge of the industry we managed to present six suitable candidates in time, including two managing directors from other firms in the same industry. A successful appointment was made. We ourselves charged the same fee for this job as we would have for one taking several weeks. That is our policy because the client is paying not so much for our time as for our know-how and hard work — and it *is* hard work — and for the ability to react quickly to a situation."

"Among the other qualities needed by a headhunter I would include, first of all, tenacity, the ability to communicate and encourage others to talk and to edit out the irrelevant from what people tell you."

Terry Ward, another search consultant, agreed with this line of approach.

"It may look like easy money", he said, "but it's like the production engineer who charged a lot of money for knowing where to hit a machine with a hammer — for "hit" read "search". And I would add that, if we're doing our job properly, it takes as much time and effort to find a man at £8,000 a year as one at £28,000."

"As we see ourselves"

Now let a selection of well known headhunters give their own views about the job and what it takes:-

"A wide industrial background, diplomacy, high level of intelligence and perception, determination and persistence."
John Anderson of John Anderson & Associates, Birmingham

"We have four basic requirements for our search consultants:

i. A senior executive with broad experience of management and industry.

ii. Good understanding of the structure, organisation and functions of management and the ability to communicate this lucidly at Board level.

iii. Mentally mature, analytical and objective, particularly in the assessment of people in a business context; warm and impressive personally; driving and resilient.

iv. Age 35-50, a graduate or professionally qualified and, desirably fluent in a European language.
John Reid of Executive Search Ltd, London S.W.3.

"We in Egon Zehnder International like to differentiate between the "headhunter" and the true executive search consultant, whose objective is to solve the client's problem and not just to bring a "head" to fill a position. This philosophy is fundamental to the firm. We therefore recruit principally from leading general management consulting firms and/or those who have a graduate business degree. In most cases our consultants have both these experiences or qualifications. This is because we believe the analytical training received both in business school and on the job in leading general management consulting firms is essential to our work. A consultant in our firm needs to be able to analyse the client's problem, to show the client that he really understands his "problem" and, in so doing, to strike up a ready rapport with his client, as well as being a man who inspires confidence in all who meet him."
R.A.B. Gowlland of Egon Zehnder International, London S.W.1.

"We are looking for the qualities of common sense, intelligence, business understanding, adaptability and an enquiring mind. Trust and integrity, of course, should be taken as read. It should also be realised that search and selection is a form of high level problem solving."
David Blamey of Spencer Stuart Management Consultants, London W.1.

"Headhunters, in my opinion, should have had general management experience, whereas a personnel manager could become a recruitment selection consultant. The headhunter must go on until he gets his man — and I don't think the general run of personnel managers are big enough people, either by function or ability, to do the job. Tenacity is the key quality."
Peter Chalkley of Sabre International Search, London, W.1.

"Two key features in the profile of "our man" are high analytical capability and the ability to create ideas in the boardroom and to influence people at that level. We recruit only management consultants, especially those who have held a senior position, for there is no room for errors in this game. The headhunter must have a trained mind, therefore we prefer graduates to non-graduates, and he should also possess selling ability."
A.E. Young of Alexander Hughes & Associates, London,W.1.

"Although most headhunters claim a catholic headhunting ability across all categories, in practice there is little doubt that knowledge of the specific market-place is an essential factor in the headhunter's competence to recruit. Apart from the usual factors such as intelligence, credibility, presentation, etc, I believe the one quality which is probably the most important is the courage to play a pro-active rather than a purely reactive role in the headhunter's relationship with the client; i.e. to be prepared to tell the client what to do, not merely to be told."
Nigel Rugman, Management Appointments Ltd, London W.1.

"Are you: tough-minded, independent or even a loner, persistent, determined or even obstinate, business-minded, commercial or even mercenary. Of good analytical or intuitive judgement, highly adaptable to people and situations, hardworking but quick to seek a solution, swift in understanding new subjects, literate, articulate, a graduate, a ready charm, a good companion and 35-40?"

"If you can honestly score yourself above 50% against this specification and think in terms of £20,000 with incentive to £40,000 and scope for equity participation in a difficult but fascinating service business, we might attract you as a partner."
Extract from one of its own recruitment advertisements by Canny Bowen & Associates of London S.W.1.

"Executive search work requires professional judgement,

sensitivity and substantial industrial experience. It requires considerable expenditure of time and efficient research and support services to provide the technical and administrative back-up on which the consultant relies.
Extract from an M.S.L. brochure

"A headhunter has to find the final piece of a jigsaw, so the best policy is to make up the rest of the jigsaw first, and this is what a headhunter should be able to do. With some companies I'll spend a week from boardroom to shopfloor before I begin to think of the person to fill the job. It is, I would stress, very hard work to do the job properly."
Terry Ward, Brook Street Executive Resources Ltd, London W.1.

"The obvious qualities are a liking for people in general, even though their attitudes may be quite alien to one's own; an ability to talk to anyone at all, to put people at their ease and to draw them out; absolute integrity; the ability to keep one's mouth shut and to respect confidence. Others that I would add, which would not necessarily be regarded as essential or even desirable by others in the business, are maturity and experience of life − I do not believe in twenty-six-year-old headhunters − and a thorough knowledge of a specialised field or fields. I am a firm believer in industry specialisation and think that the most effective headhunters are those who really know the field concerned through having worked in it themselves. The generalist can only go so far and then often comes to a dead stop where the candidate can probably tell him more about the insides of a job than the interviewer himself knows. (I have in years past been a candidate in precisely this sort of position.)"
Roger Stacey, Astron Appointments Ltd, London W.8.

"A search consultant should be the kind of person to whom a client will unbare his soul and who is also able to put a candidate at his ease. Broad management experience is also highly desirable − for example, we recruit our consultants

from leading firms such as Shell or I.C.I. The job itself demands hard and concentrated work. The consultant with an assignment is on his own with a deadline to meet, as often as not."
Peter Prentice, Tyzack & Partners, London W.1.

"Even though our field is computing and engineering, we make a point of studying the candidate's personality closely for fitting in is just as important in this sector as in general management. Indeed, I would say that human and managerial qualities are more important than technical qualifications. The search man himself should have a "high visibility factor" and be ready to meet candidates early in the morning or late in the evening, if necessary."
Michael Gernat, Electronic Computing and Management Appointments Ltd, Royston, Herts.

What is one to make of all this? It is probably better to leave the reader to sift out his own conclusions rather than attempt the impossible task of compiling an identikit word picture of the "compleat headhunter", especially as it is clear that no such creature exists. There seems, however, to be a more or less consensus view that a headhunter should be over thirty-five, have managerial experience in commerce or industry and the ability to get people to talk about themselves (which is not necessarily the same thing as liking people). For good measure, there should be an aptitude for hard work and a trained mind. In my experience, a keenly developed sense of business can be taken as read; headhunters may not lack compassion but they do not run charities. Here, an overall picture emerges which falls far short of the superman portrait which would result simply by adding up the various qualities mentioned in the foregoing extracts.

There is also a fairly common belief among headhunters that small is beautiful, and it is certainly true that, even among the large international partnerships, individual units or offices are usually of quite modest size — with perhaps five to six consultants. The main argument put forward in support of this pattern is that a small team is more flexible, can respond more quickly to changing needs and circumstances and is able to offer the client a far more personal service — the same argument, in fact, that is used to support the notion of small management units generally. Much depends of course on the attitude and character of the managing partner, on whether he is a genuine delegator or prefers to manipulate most of the strings himself.

To round off this profile of today's headhunters, a view from the other side of the Atlantic is apposite. Writing as early as the summer of 1978, Roger Kenny of Spencer Stuart & Associates claimed that the search profession was already attracting "people who enjoyed its demanding pace and creative challenge."

"These are students of business", he continued, "who have people-handling skills related to identifying and appraising executives. They are strong communicators who are sensitive to corporation nuances. They are mentors who have advised industry leaders to change companies and even to change careers. The best have taken a long-term view of their chosen profession and enjoy being measured by the business results of their clients."

This point was brought home to me in the course of interviewing for this book when George Harris of Canny Bowen & Associates told me that he had "just made his first millionaire". In this case, he was referring to someone he had placed a few years previously in a top executive job.

Anyhow, it may be easy to talk about "demanding pace and creative challenge" but what do these mean in the context of headhunting? How, precisely, does a headhunter earn his bread?

Anatomy of a search

"A lot of people seem to think", said George Harris of Canny Bowen, "that the headhunter just swans around, knows a lot of people, talks a bit and — hey presto! — produces Superman like a rabbit out of a hat.

There are harder ways of making a living, it is true, but headhunting is not quite as easy as that. Making allowance for the fact that no two businesses are identical and that some assignments are more difficult than others, a typical search job will consist of four key steps — namely: agreeing the job specification with the client; undertaking the search for candidates; screening the candidates and preparing the short list; advising on the job offer and follow-up. Each of these steps can of course be further broken down, so that some headhunters may think of a typical search assignment as consisting of six or more steps. It should also be noted that three of the steps outlined apply also in the case of selection consultants, the only difference being that step number two "undertaking the search for candidates" is replaced by attracting applicants through planned advertisements. One of the current metaphors is that the search man uses a rifle where the selection man fires a shotgun — or a rod and line instead of a trawl — while another important distinction is that the former deals with people whose interest is sought while the latter deals with applicants. Hence the selection consultant is in a more "dominant" posture as regards the people whom he sees in respect of an appointment.

Here, however, we look primarily at what is involved in "pure" headhunting, as it were; that is, at a search assignment.

Agreeing the job specification

Many headhunters see this as the key element in the whole process. Any conscientious search consultant will not blindly accept the client's description of the vacancy in question or of the kind of man he wants and the salary and conditions on offer. He will also want to find out more about the client's business, about its profit performance and prospects, its management structure and what can best be described as the "group personality" of the executive team. Almost without exception headhunters look for executives whose personal chemistry will enable them to "fit in" (a favourite piece of jargon) with the client's way of doing things — and this applies whether the headhunter is looking for a high flyer or a good number two.

"The search process", in the view of Roger Kenny, "is started by clearly defining the nature of the assignment. In fact, one of the services of a recruiting firm is to help with corporate decision making regarding priorities early in the search process. Not only does this prevent misunderstandings later in the search, but the setting of priorities also helps to bring the client's business and needs clearly in focus. Without this phase, both sides are crap-shooting that an "ideal" candidate can be found to fit the perfectly defined position."

All this is made much easier of course where the head-hunter has an ongoing relationship with the client firm, hence has a sharper appreciation of its needs and management style — naturally such a relationship is also sought because it implies repeat business.

Here are a few further comments by leading U.K. and international headhunters on this aspect of a search assignment.

"We feel very strongly that the original job definition is crucial. Get this right and the search is easier."

"We spend several hours, or as long as is necessary, with our client in order both to assimilate thoroughly the technical requirements of the job and to gain a "feel" for the client company's politics and relationships. We would also say that an important factor in utilizing our services is the acceptance of our advice on the construction of the job specification and salary."

"The headhunter is brought in to solve the client's problem, so the job specification is normally drawn up in collaboration with the client, and we amplify this by a very full proposal letter which runs to at least seven or eight pages. We invariably draw up the actual specification ourselves after discussions with the client. The salary, in our experience is also fairly flexible."

"The job specification is discussed very thoroughly indeed, unless it is (a) a company we already know well or (b) a very straightforward role to be filled. Yes, we are quite often instrumental in causing the client to amend his original job specification and salary-level (not always upward either!)"

"We start all our assignments from scratch and require only a pad and a pencil to get under way." (The interviewee here is the head of a firm which does not keep records as a matter of policy.) "For example, one of our consultants who had never been to South East Asia successfully obtained six multi-national candidates as a result of three weeks research out of our London office followed by three weeks on the ground based in an hotel room in Singapore. We can take a brief in half an hour or we may spend half a day. The average is about 90 minutes. We do advise clients about the job and the salary."

"We are intensively involved in the job specification — we will challenge, comment and re-write, if need be, including action on the remuneration offered. To give one example, we were called in by a textile manufacturer to find a new sales and marketing director, but we came to the conclusion, after carrying out an analysis, that the present incumbent compared favourably with any others we were likely to get. So we looked at the activity and the packaging of the product, and discovered that this latter was the territory of the managing director. Our ultimate recommendation was that this become the remit of the existing marketing director. So we in fact said 'Don't appoint a new man at all'. We often recommend our clients to promote internally."

Quite a number of search firms make the same recommendation after "tasting" the job, the company and its culture. "First, look in the client's manor itself" is in fact part of the conventional wisdom of the headhunting world. As for the inflexible client who refuses to alter his original specification, there are many headhunters who aver that they will not handle jobs which are "wrong" in their view, or where (as is by no means unknown) the would-be client expects a superman for peanuts. Like any businessmen, however, headhunters are reluctant to let income slip through their fingers — and in any case the man who pays the piper calls the tune, or at least the arrangement of the music — so most discussions on job specification end in compromise but with the client having the major say.

The search proper

A number of methods may be employed by the headhunter to track down the people he is looking for. He will of course (i) exploit his own knowledge and experience of industry and (ii) will probably reinforce this by consulting his own records. Further help may come from special "contacts" — people with a special knowledge of the industry concerned or of who's who in a variety of specialist functions from financial directors to boffins. Fourthly, our headhunter may decide to advertise as well as conduct a private search; at one time, this was considered almost to be breaking some unwritten law, but no longer.

Every headhunting firm, even the few who do not keep records, should have a wide knowledge of the territory in which they operate. Indeed, it is difficult to avoid acquiring such knowledge unless they are idiots with remarkably short memories, in which case politics would probably be a more suitable career. The successful search consultants, to quote A.E. Young of Alexander Hughes & Associates, "will have wandered around industry for years and made notes on the people who struck them as being impressive; they have been listening to gossip and have been assiduously pumping their business contacts, they read papers and magazines, and of course they get a constant stream of willing victims letting it coyly be known that they might be open to offers." Mounting the search is thus much easier for the headhunter than it would be for the company conducting its own quest for top executive talent.

The way in which a search consultancy keeps its records

is of course infinitely variable. A few of the larger firms have gone over to computers, thereby vastly extending capacity and speed of access, but the majority still seem to manage quite adequately with manual systems. Much more important is the judgement behind the decision to put someone in a data bank and the manner in which the track record and qualities of the individual concerned are classified.

As stated, some headhunters eschew record keeping as a matter of policy. A leading example is Executive Search Ltd of Knightsbridge, one of the first in the field in the United Kingdom. "We do not keep files because they date too quickly", claimed its managing director, John Reid, "and it is quicker and more reliable to locate and identify potential candidates by researching current performance and achievement." This contrasts sharply with the view of Eurosurvey Ltd, whose director, Anthony Langdon, emphasized that "our whole operation is based upon massive research, and, initially, we will contact anything up to 300 people — i.e. contact by telephone." All of which mainly goes to underline that, like the great detectives of fiction, each group of headhunters has its own methods.

Invariably, the initial contact with potential candidates is made by telephone, and here again headhunters are by no means unanimous. Some prefer to call their quarry in the evening to ensure privacy and when the "target" is likely to be more relaxed and the person contacted more able to give consideration to a career change proposition. Others, among them Peter Prentice of Tyzack & Partners, prefer to contact a prospect at his place of business. "He may resent our contacting him in the evening when he could be relaxing with friends or helping his children with their homework", he explained. "We prefer to be more direct, as members of a profession which is becoming increasingly accepted all the time. We ask if it's convenient to talk to him and, if so, we go ahead and explain the purpose of our call." Such details may or may not be important, but they reflect the "style" of the consultancy.

The use of special contacts within an industry or managerial circle can obviously provide a headhunter with, as it were, a head's start in many an assignment. Such contacts, says A.E. Young, as "know where the bright young men are . . . and when a reputation is not wholly deserved. So when the assignment to fill a job comes in, headhunters already know which companies, trade associations and independent advisers they should turn to for help . . ."

"Quite often the client will explain that he already has his eye on a candidate and all he wants from the headhunter is a few other runners to make it a race. It is amusing to note just how often in such cases the hotly tipped favourite comes in a sorry third. Not because the company picked an unsuitable man – just that the wider you look, the more likely you are to come up with a good candidate and a more balanced point of view."

And once again, Roger Kenny with the American view:
"One of the myths of executive recruiting is that search firms have elaborate file systems which enable them quickly to identify the leading candidates. The universe of potential candidates is much too large and dynamic to rely on files. The most important resource of a recruiter is his industry specialists, or sources. These are the so-called "deans", very knowledgeable contacts who must be cultivated personally by recruiters."

Even so, files are useful and are used extensively, especially by headhunters specialising in a given sector and by selection consultants. Kenny is right, however, to stress that they are not the most important tool in the headhunter's kit because most of the assignments he handles are too specific to be filled satisfactorily without a personal search.

Constructing a short list
This part of the search process is likewise primarily a matter of hard work plus judgement. Headhunters seldom employ any novel gimmicks or techniques in whittling down the candidates to be presented to the client to a manageable size – probably three or four, and rarely, if at all, more

than six. True, some search and selection firms favour the use of intelligence and psychological testing, while graphology is very popular in Europe and astrology in France and the Far East. For the most part, however, headhunters in Britain tend to rely on common sense, experience and the track record of the candidate when sorting out the sheep from the goats. As already noted "fitting in" is regarded as a cardinal virtue, and the quest is by no means always for a high flyer. Job knowledge and experience, by definition, is already present, or why would the candidate have been searched in the first place. Nine out of ten firms have CV (*curriculum vitae*) forms of their own devising, but very few contain 'clever' questions or ask for esoteric or original opinions. Overall, the approach is systematic and pragmatic — conservative, basically — but this need be no bad thing. In the words of one headhunter:

"As to the filling in of application forms, our own view is that, firstly, any idiot can fill in little boxes on a *pro forma*, and the information given is therefore hardly productive, while asking candidates to fill in such forms is merely an irritant to them." Bearing in mind that a man who has been searched can hardly be described as an applicant, another headhunter emphasized, "I discuss, I don't interview." A third said: "We prefer to have a candidate's concise personal history on our own two-sided A4 format before discussing his interest and suitability."

Judgement and experience may be the most important assets for a headhunter, but first impressions of candidates who have been filtered out for further screening may have to be confirmed. A track record may read just a little too well, or a candidate may have been a little too eager to be headhunted in the first place. Nor is it always easy to find out whether a candidate is prized by his existing employer or has become a downright nuisance; if the latter, colleagues may say the nicest things about him in the hope that some rival firm will spirit him away.

The job offer and follow-up

Whilst the client must make the final decision as to who is appointed, most headhunters stress that an assignment does not and should not end with the creation and presentation of a short list. It would be idle to pretend that this golden rule is universally observed (in any case some clients insist on taking over completely at the short list stage) but some typical comments bear out the principle:-

"We always present our candidates personally and remain during the first meeting with the client. Thereafter we are at the disposal of both sides to give independent advice or assistance. The final decision is always taken by the client and the candidate."

"With selection, we get involved up to the reference checking stage, and the trend today is towards making a recommendation. With search, the approach is quite different, and we often process one candidate at a time." (This from M.S.L., probably the largest selection consultancy in the United Kingdom.)

"We act to the point of the candidate's effective operation with his new company. We have no forms to complete of any significance and we reckon to be judged on performance after eighteen months to two years."

"We take the assignment right the way through to the taking up of references. We don't use forms but we might ask for a CV. We're very keen on follow-up as well because it's the right thing to do and because it can lead to repeat business. For example, thirteen years ago we acted for a client with a £50 million turnover which today has risen to £500 million, and there are only two people on the main board whom we haven't placed."

"Probably the most important role fulfilled by the consultant is as an intermediary at the final negotiating stages, and to

44

leave the client unaided at this point would be tantamount to incompetence."

"Our service continues not only beyond the short list stage, but also through to interviews (we are always present at the initial interviews) and to the integration of the executive into his new company. I should stress that he is not an applicant but someone who is being brought in to solve the client's problem and who has to be persuaded that the job is worth doing."

The above observations at least make it clear that most executive search assignments fade away into successful completion rather than come to an abrupt halt; we are talking of course about assignments that end in a satisfactory placement, because the professional recruiter has his failures as well as his successes. The job can linger on for any of a number of reasons: the consultant, for instance may have to act as an intermediary when everything else has been settled except salary and other conditions of employment, or he may choose to get in touch with the client and/or the successful candidate some time after the appointment to find out how the new man is settling in. Or, again, a successful placement often leads to repeat business, so in one sense a successful assignment never ends.

One point which struck me while interviewing for this chapter was that, whilst much was said about duties and responsibilities towards clients, only two or three of the headhunters with whom I spoke mentioned anything about their obligations to candidates. To be fair, perhaps they thought this was implicit in remarks about refusing to handle assignments where, in their view, the job specification and salary were wrong. One of their number did, however, stress the importance of "not selling the candidate a pup".

"It's bad for everyone", he went on, "including the consultant. Therefore the candidate's interest is vital, and we ourselves recommend a post only if we think it is to the candidate's advantage." Among others who endorsed this policy were a few who added that, in time, a candidate whose interests had been respected could well become a client.

It should be reiterated that most of what has been written here about the methods and the attitudes of search consultants should in theory apply also to the selection industry, where of course the skills and sensitivities of recruitment are equally relevant. Whether or not it all adds up to good value for money is a question discussed in Chapter Five.

Role of the client
Implicit in all that has been written in this chapter is the need for a good relationship between the headhunter and client — a creative two-way process, as some recruiters call it — one based on respect, trust and understanding. This is certainly the consensus view among both search and selection consultancies, but it is by no means the unanimous opinion among potential users. The BIM/IPM survey quoted some typical misgivings among firms in general:

"You run the risk with executive search of giving them access to the whole of your structure — this can be dangerous."

"I would be frightened if I got someone from the headhunters that six months or a year later they were going to be approached by the same people."

"Headhunters are not used because I don't believe in the ethics of headhunters."

The headhunter may throw up his arms in despair at what he sees as antediluvian attitudes such as the above. Nevertheless such attitudes persist and still — fairly or otherwise — tarnish the image of the outside recruiter.

The headhunter's answer to the charges of being expensive, ineffective and/or untrustworthy (looked at more fully in Chapter Five) must be (a) to eliminate any causes for such suspicions and (b) to persuade the client of the importance of genuine cooperation and flexibility. "The client can best help the consultant", says Nigel Rugman, "by being absolutely candid and by realising that the amount of time and energy he is prepared to invest is directly related to the quality of the end product he will receive. The size of the company or the type of industry has little bearing on the subject; what matters is the objectivity with which the qualities required in the individual are identified."

David Blamey of Spencer Stuart Management Consultants sees it a little differently. "Very large companies produce communication difficulties", he said, "while very small ones are tempted to recruit "big company people" who may be expert but who are ineffective in such a different environment."

A third headhunter stressed that the client needs to keep in close touch not only with the consultant but with the candidates as well, and to make sure that "he treats them as senior executives and not as low level applicants for jobs. He must therefore behave courteously and follow up reasonably rapidly with interviews so that the candidates are not kept waiting too long." Yet another thought that the client should "come clean about the disadvantages of the job" — e.g. possible resentment inside the firm against an "outsider" — as well as about the good points.

"Speaking very generally", he continued, "the larger firms tend to create problems of delay — too many channels to be gone through, too much bureaucracy and too much complacency, leading to the loss of strong candidates. The problems arising with small firms are more often caused by the personality and attitudes of a specific individual — usually the chairman and/or chief executive."

Further views on the constructive client were that he should be flexible over age and salary and should not delay unduly in coming to a decision. In view of one well known consultant (who on this point understandably wishes not to be quoted by name) "Multi-nationals tend to make the most difficult clients, especially American ones, whereas on the whole we find U.K. companies much better to deal with. They are quicker and more pragmatic." Another simply contented himself with the observation that "clients can be and usually are difficult for reasons too numerous to list in a short answer."

Sifting the various comments on this aspect of the head-hunter's work, it is obvious that the professional recruiter knows what he wants of the client but is still a long way from getting it. Obviously, he must have frankness and a modicum of information about the company and its performance, plans and people, but where such information is meted out very sparingly the reason may lie in the client's lack of confidence in the profession generally. There was a time in the not too distant past when the recruitment industry had more than its fair share of "cowboys", of quick buck merchants and blatant poachers. Things may have changed since the recession, but not every client, especially those who use headhunters out of desperation, is aware of this, and the necessary confidence can come only from the search and selection consultants themselves.

One thing, however, which the client *can* learn for himself is that, at most, a good headhunter can find only the best available man, and he should appreciate that top talent cannot be attracted by rock-bottom rates. This is perhaps the hardest lesson of all. Hope springs eternal in the board-room as well as in the betting shop.

4
Specialisation?

Had the late Professor Cyril Joad ever had the opportunity to contemplate the executive recruitment industry (which came some years after his time) he would have undoubtedly replied to the above question with the comment: "It all depends what you mean by specialisation."

Looking at the activity in the round, it is clear that the industry offers both specialisation by function and by activity, and also that many consultancies (search as well as selection teams) will specialise or "generalise" as the opportunity occurs. As one well known headhunter told me, and I do not think any irony was intended, "we specialise in finance, marketing, general management, retail, senior sales management and banking/City appointments. We are also increasingly concerned with the development of a consultancy service to find senior expatriate executives for Hong Kong." Finding executives to take up overseas appointments was in fact claimed as a form of specialisation by many consultants. So too was the search for directors and chief executives, for general managers and non-executive directors; this last activity is becoming an increasingly important brief in the portfolios of several leading firms of headhunters. One such added that "no successful headhunter can afford to be weak in the City establishment sector, for the people with top jobs in their gift tend to have strong links with finance." The following is another comment on how the

49

term "specialisation" is interpreted by some of the big boys in the industry:

"As one of the largest firms in the world in its field, we do not specialise in any particular market in functional terms. We do, however, specialise "at senior executive level" — in other words, most of our work is to advise on appointments at board level or the equivalent. A substantial percentage (perhaps one third) is at chairman or chief executive level."

However, what most readers will understand by the term "specialisation" will be, does the consultancy operate in any specific market — for example, computing and electronics, engineering, agriculture, banking, insurance, hotel and catering, PR and advertising, publishing, transport and freighting, and so on and on? The answer, especially if we include selection as well as search consultants, is a most emphatic "Yes". This much is patently clear merely from the names of consultancies listed in Robert Baird's directory, *The Executive Grapevine*. Examples include: Agricultural Appointments Ltd, Banking Personnel, Building Associates, Finance Recruitment, Hotel World, Malla Technical Services Group, OCC Computer Personnel, SMR Sales & Market Recruiters Ltd, and Transport Management Services Ltd.

Job knowledge or in-breeding?

Clearly, then, there is no shortage of 'specialists' in the recruitment industry, giving point to Roger Stacey's comment that "the generalist can only go so far and then often comes to a dead stop, which is why I believe the most effective headhunters are those who really know the field concerned through having worked in it themselves." A less sanguine view is taken by John Reid of Executive Search Ltd who claimed: "With specialisation by industry, you end up by taking from Peter to pay Paul. The search consultancy should give an undertaking not to take away from its own clients for at least two years, so it ends up with nowhere to look. In this way you can be left with the people you know rather than with the right people. With functional specialisation, on the other hand, there is a danger of looking at the professional standpoint rather than at company needs. For example, a first-class financial executive should be sought by the non-specialist headhunter, for the latter should be looking for a financial specialist who has it in him to become a chief executive."

The danger of ending up "with the people you know rather than with the right people" goes a long way to explaining why, among specialist headhunters, selection techniques tend to be just as important as the search process, and frequently more important. Selection based on national or selective advertising is a much more effective method than search for discovering fresh talent, and thus guards against the danger of "incestuous" recruitment. Again, headhunters specialising in one or more related industries invariably charge lower fees than search men operating in the higher reaches of management. For instance, I have been quoted instances of anything between 5% and 10% by a recruiter in the hotel and catering and transport fields, from which it is self-evident that what may be termed "classical search" simply cannot feature in the process, or else the consultancies concerned would go bankrupt before they had compiled their first shortlists.

"We charge 12½% of the annual salary", said Peggy Wingardh of Lyon & Brandfield Recruitment Ltd, who specialise in PR and advertising agency appointments, "coming down to 10% after the first two placements with any client in any one calendar year. We advertise mainly in the trade publications – in our case, *Campaign* and *PR Bulletin* – but before that we make a point of holding tough discussions with the client as regards the job and the conditions of employment."

A different approach is favoured by Fleet Personnel Selection, a consultancy operating in the freight and transport field.

"We charge 5% of the expected gross salary as a registration fee", explained Mike Millington, the firm's managing director, "plus a further 10% if and when an appointment is made. I would add that, initially, many of our clients have fixed ideas, but we try to encourage them to look at the candidate's potential as well as at his actual experience, and at the contribution the person concerned could make to our client's future."

Specialist headhunters also tend to operate further downmarket than the leading search consultancies, and as a result will handle appointments attracting considerably lower salaries. Many search consultants, for example, will not act in the case of appointments commanding salaries below £15,000 a year — perhaps £20,000 or even £25,000 — whereas the consultant in a specialist field will often consider vacancies quoted at £8,000 or even less. At the lower end of the scale, it is indeed difficult to know at which point the term "selection consultancy" should be replaced by "employment agency". In saying this, I should stress that I am not making a value judgement — "Some of my best friends are employment agents", so to speak — merely drawing attention to the fact that the generic activity we call the "recruitment industry" has its own class structure.

Managerial qualities sought

The main message which comes across from headhunters specialising in a given industry is that, job knowledge apart, they tend to look for the same qualities as their "generalist" colleagues. Which is to say, that they look primarily for candidates with a managerial track record, for people who will "fit in" with the client's team and who understand the profit motive and are likely to make a contribution in this area. For example, Brian Worthington, formerly group personnel manager of Grand Metropolitan Hotels and now manager of the Hotel World Division of Bastable Personnel Services, points out that almost every job in the hotel industry from hall porter to head chef involves a high degree of self-motivation, so the hotel manager must himself have this quality to an even greater degree. "Again", he added, "the costings have to be so precise in this field that management flair is a No. 1 priority — not to mention that to a large extent the job and one's private life are often inseparable. Therefore we need not only managerial skills but social skills and a sense of vocation as well."

Mike Millington of Fleet Personnel Selection made more or less the same point.

"The client's wishes are what counts in the end of course, but all too often his thinking is boxed in by past experience, and he may think primarily in terms of people with knowledge of the field — be it forwarding agent, haulier, running a warehouse, distribution or running a fleet of trucks — and forget all about managerial skills. We try, if you like, to get him out of this box, by encouraging him to think more widely and consider potential as well as experience. For example, one of our clients was looking for a sales executive to work in the container leasing field. He was not able to find anyone suitable within this particular activity, but we were able to persuade him that temperament and personality were far more important than actual knowledge of the containers market, and that we could well recruit someone with the necessary qualities from another area of industrial product marketing. We were able to find just such a person, a self-starter, numerate and capable of initiating business on his own and able to deal with customers, including the difficult ones."

For his part, Mike Gernat, head of Electronic Computer and Management Appointments Ltd, who was himself headhunted into the recruitment industry then later set up his own business, thinks that human and managerial qualities should take priority over technical skills and experience even in such fields as computing and electronics. "Like any individual", he said, "companies have personalities, so we make a point of studying the human personality to see if the candidate is likely to fit in — or, if you like, is capable of interfacing — with the company. For that reason we also pay special attention to any managerial track record. You may think we attach a lot of importance to the business of fitting in, but it matters a great deal in the micro-processing industry where companies tend to be small and flexible and the management team simply have to get along with each other."

Gernat, whose company is based on Royston, Hertfordshire, makes the point that his office location has not made the slightest difference to company profitability — "In fact," he claims, "it's quite a good sales gimmick." He will handle appointments carrying salaries from £5,000 a year to £25,000 a year, and charges 12½% of salary as a fee. "It may not amount to much in the case of a junior programmer," he said, "but if you get eight to ten a month, then you begin to talk money."

Non-executive directors
One kind of specialism which is beginning to attract a growing number of the leading headhunters is the search for non-executive or "independent" directors. This type of appointment, according to a special report in the *Bank of England Quarterly Bulletin* of December 1979 was then finding "growing acceptance" among Britain's top 1,000 companies, and, if anything, the trend has continued from strength to strength. At the time of the report, the proportion of top companies employing three or more such directors had risen from just over one third to just over one half, while the number without any independent directors at all had dwindled from 25% to 12%.

Another survey published in the same year made the point that, although one in four of Britain's largest manufacturing companies had a merchant bank director on its board as a non-executive, the trend was gradually changing against such appointments because of the dangers of a conflict of interest. The same survey showed, however, that the leading U.K. companies were drawing nearly 60% of their independent directors from among senior executive directors of other companies, people employed full-time elsewhere in industry. In the case of medium-sized and smaller concerns, the proportion was as high as 75 to 80%. This helps to explain why headhunters these days are well advised to check whether people they approach come from the same companies as non-executive directors on clients' boards.

Anyhow, the contention of headhunters working in this field is that independent directors fulfill a very necessary function but that most boards are by no means as efficient or creative as they should be. According to Spencer Stuart Management Consultants, companies should ask three basic questions about this type of director: (1) how many outsiders should a board carry? (2) how much time should they devote, and (3) most importantly, what sort of background should they have?

As regards the first of these questions, it is worth noting that in the United States company boards are mostly non-executive, with anything from 80 to 90% of directors being outside independents, whereas by contrast in the United Kingdom there are many sizeable and well known enterprises which have never admitted an "outsider" to the boardroom. There can, however, be no precise answer to the question of "how many?". Obviously it depends on the company and its structure, but the Bank of England figures suggest that there should be at least three non-executive directors on the board of a major concern, while about six or seven on a total board of twelve would seem to be a workable maximum.

As to time spent in the role of independent director, Spencer Stuart Consultants says that the general consensus seems to be that ten per cent of total working time — or about two days a month — is typical. More than this, it could be argued, might affect the objectivity of his thinking, which is one of the main reasons for appointing an independent director in the first place.

In the matter of fees, the Bank of England survey revealed that these vary widely, from £250 to £10,000 a year, while some companies were still paying (in 1979) the same £2,000 as they were paying ten years earlier. At the time of the survey, however, fees for the most part ranged between £2,000 and £6,000 a year, which is more or less the situation today as well.

Thirdly, what type of animal should a non-executive director be? A few there are, it is true, who still seem to be able to make a career of the job, sitting on the boards of several companies being smooth and charming and perhaps conferring a touch of prestige and harmless platitudes. It is they who provoke so much scepticism among financial journalists about this type of appointment. Then there is the well meaning and conscientious retired pundit, anything perhaps from an accountant to an academic, conservative, timid, a bit out of touch and not very effective despite his earnest endeavours.

Without expecting paragons, the type of person thought to make the most effective independent director today is someone combining a track record in general management with specialist skills in, say, finance, production, marketing or industrial relations. Such a person should also be able to analyse and communicate ideas and lessons gleaned from practical experience. However, anyone can draw up a list of virtues which make a non-executive director worth his salt; those quoted most frequently are independence of judgement and an objective approach to problems, giving support and counsel to the chief executive, providing specific expertise and contributing to the strategic planning of the enterprise.

It quickly becomes clear from all this that here is an important new market for headhunters, one that can not only make a substantial contribution to profits but also helps the headhunter to develop an on-going type of relationship with the client company and gives him an insight into the personality and structure of its top management. Spencer Stuart Management Consultants with offices all over the world, is particularly active in this field, and so too is Tyzack & Partners which operates a special scheme for the recruitment of non-executive directors in conjunction with the Institute of Directors; these, however, are only two names among several.

As already mentioned, financial journalists do not always

entertain the same enthusiasm for the post as does the headhunting fraternity, but this will surprise no one. Paradoxically, if the headhunters operating in this particular sector, or specialism, do their jobs properly, then maybe — to paraphrase Oliver Goldsmith — journalists who come to sneer will remain to pray.

Much ado about nothing?

There may be disagreement over whether or not a headhunter should specialise, but there is certainly no controversy; it is not a topic which raises the professional blood pressure, and in any case I would like to know by what criteria recruiters who spend their working lives looking for top executives for general management or financial posts can be said not to specialise. I am reminded of Sherlock Holmes' description of the activities of his brother, Mycroft: "Every man is a specialist, my dear Watson, and Mycroft's is omniscience." I am not of course hinting that headhunters are in such a state of grace, but by definition they work in a specific sector of a particular area of management.

What many of them do contend, however, is that by concentrating on finding, say, engineers, computer programmers, farm managers or PR executives, the professional recruiters run the risk of catching a financial cold during times of severe recession, in contrast with the generalists labouring away in the higher management vineyard.

In my view, this is an exaggeration. True, the recession is affecting the recruitment industry as a whole, but some sectors much more than others. For example, some employment agencies placing clerical, secretarial and other office trades have had to live with a substanstantial cut in turnover, and some headhunting firms have likewise had their profits trimmed, but few selection and search consultancies have been seriously threatened as a result of the recession. In the nature of things, this is what one would expect. Headhunters by definition are supposed to go for the best available, and only in a total economic collapse is the demand for real talent and rare skills likely to vanish. Thus, amid growing numbers of redundant executives, most of them in staff jobs, and the number of unemployed in America, Britain and Western Europe going up by millions, the demand for engineers, computing staff, accountants, scientists, industrial chemists and so on continues to be buoyant. Even the advertising industry, one of the first sectors to suffer in a recession, according to legend, has remained in remarkably good condition, if a trifle leaner in some areas.

The distinction between the specialist recruiter and the headhunter working at boardroom level may be very real, however, in terms of attitude and approach. Whilst the former may think in terms of professional qualifications in the case of a technical or managerial appointment, the latter may be looking for a future chief executive, and neither might be wholly right or wrong. Yet here too any differences are more likely to relate to the individual rather than to what it says on the firm's letterhead.

In any case, despite recession and accusations of poaching, cowboys and exorbitant costs, and the overall bias in favour of home-grown talent, the headhunting industry is poised for further growth, whether the quest be for some high flyer builder of business empires or for a designer of printed circuits.

Besides, if he is any good, an element of specialisation is bound to infiltrate the work of any headhunter as a result of repeat assignments and long association with certain clients. Repeat work, moreover, gives the headhunter the confidence and security he needs along with the job knowledge to turn in a good performance consistently. Let it not be forgotten that the "stars" of the recruitment industry are just as lonely and vulnerable as anyone else.

5

Value for Money

According to the BIM/IPM 1980 survey on Selecting Managers, only 14% of companies in the United Kingdom use the services of selection consultants and even fewer — an estimated 4% — take their recruitment problems to the executive search industry. However, the fact that the vast majority of employers prefer to home grow their executive talent, or use direct advertising certainly does not add up to a watertight case against head-hunting — here, I should remind readers, the term is used to cover both selection and search.

As we have seen, search is concerned almost exclusively with top level appointments and selection likewise operates at a fairly senior level, so in one sense the figures quoted are no more or less than one would expect. It is right and proper that firms should home grow their own talent through a mix of management development programmes and actually doing the job (almost a heresy, this latter in the 1960s). Internal development and promotion is generally thought to be good for morale and to help in the motivation of employees, as well as conforming with the "better the devil you know" principle. Other advantages are that it provides the basis for a career structure within the enterprise, for the systematic assessment of individuals and makes much easier the planning of the management succession. There are of course disadvantages in the policy too, such as too much inbreeding, staleness and lack of new ideas and the

59

stirring up of jealousy and resentment where one colleague is promoted over another. Yet at least three-quarters of British companies seem to prefer internal recruitment and promotion to any other, though most of them will have secured their "raw material" in the first place through advertising in the national, local and/or specialist press.

The pitfalls of inbreeding and (perhaps) staleness are avoided when a company decides to call in a headhunter, but that does not mean that talent-hungry businesses are as yet beating paths to the search consultants' doors. Large sections of commerce and industry still think of headhunters as rather smooth customers whose fees and expenses are "enormous". In fact, nearly half the respondents to the BIM/IPM survey rated national press advertising as the most effective channel of external recruitment and the professional registers as the least effective. Over half the companies taking part also expressed themselves dissatisfied with executive search, not, be it added, because of the poor quality of the candidates presented — quite the reverse, in fact, both in the case of search and selection consultants — but in terms of what the survey called "cost effectiveness". This, presumably, boils down to the conviction among clients that they could have recruited just as well by other methods and at much smaller cost.

What is the headhunter's answer to this?

One Midlands firm of headhunters whom I asked about the advantages of recruiting through a search consultancy replied that these were "self-evident". That may well be so, as far as the profession is concerned, but it is not very edifying to those outside it and anyway is hardly the kind of response likely to win clients and influence others. I much prefer the answer of Roger Stacey (Astron Appointments Ltd) who wrote:

"The selection consultant is often chosen in preference to a personnel department, in my view, because —

i.   smaller companies often don't have a formal personnel department, anyway.

ii. recruitment is only one aspect of a personnel department's total function and often their other duties — e.g. in union negotiations, fixing of salary scales, etc. — don't allow them enough time to deal adequately with a key recruitment exercise.

iii. the consultant is not parochial in his outlook, as so many personnel departments inevitably are.

iv. the consultant can approach anyone informally and without embarrassment, and potential candidates will open up far more readily to an intermediary than to a company interviewer.

v. depth of knowledge of the industry or specialism concerned is another key advantage.

In the case of the search consultant, to this list of virtues must be added that of of confidentiality. This weighs very heavily with company chief executives and other directors; some believe in fact that this is the only advantage the headhunter can offer.

Anyhow, from talking with a number of leading headhunters, I would say that in general they claim five key selling points for their role, as follows:-

1. They save the client's top management team valuable time and effort.

2. The headhunter's service provides confidentiality. Very often headhunters handle assignments known only to the chief executive and the main board of the client firm.

3. It also preserves the confidentiality of the candidates, many of whom may not wish it to be known that they are looking for another job — or a "career change", as some prefer to put it — until at least the short list stage.

4. The headhunter knows where to start and can bring to an assignment what one of them described as "external objectivity, market perspective and experience". Interviewing skill is another asset claimed.

5. A competent headhunter will top and tail an assignment, first by advising on the job profile and by acting as an honest broker and adviser over pay and perks in the final stages. Many also practise systematic follow-up, checking on how the person chosen is settling in at his new company and on the contribution he is making.

Let us look at these in turn.

The saving of top management time is one of those phrases which rolls so glibly off the tongue that it is hard to believe it is true in many cases. Senior executives in any type of undertaking ought to be fully stretched most of the time, though this should not imply they should have no time for management development or planning the succession. Yet it is also a fact that very few senior managers have any formal training in recruiting; most of them rely on knowledge of the job and the organisation, on hunch and experience, and few make use of any other selection technique than the interview. It can be argued, then, that top management is much better advised to concentrate on what it is already doing than to start specialising in recruitment.

Again, it is true that many small and medium-sized companies have nothing like a fully-fledged personnel department, especially one capable of handling a top-level appointment. Even where an adequate personnel department exists, it is absurd that the personnel director should be expected to recruit perhaps his own boss. In any case the modern personnel department deals with so many activities — anything from safety and welfare to wage negotiations and pension schemes — that few of them have the time or the experience to mount a systematic search assignment. "There is no substitute for a systematic search throughout the industry", claims R.A.B. Gowlland of Egon Zehnder International, "and clearly the client's own personnel department is unable to do this. Its members are not skilled in executive search which is, in the leading firms, a highly professional operation."

Anyhow, many leading headhunting firms now believe that personnel departments are themselves coming to realise that recruitment is only one of their many responsibilities and that the outside specialist is likely to be more competent in this area. "A good personnel executive will delegate to the specialist recruiting consultant", claims John Reid of Executive Search Ltd. "Besides, a personnel executive cannot undertake a search, in our view, because anonymity is an essential ingredient of the whole exercise." Garry Long of M.S.L. concedes that confidentiality and anonymity are important but no longer crucial because "it is now accepted that a high flyer will be looking ahead."

Even so, there may be very good reasons for a firm to conceal the fact that it is looking for a chief executive or a finance, marketing or production director, or whoever. Competitor firms can learn a great deal from "decoding" even anonymous advertisements put together by the most experienced selection consultants; so too, presumably, can the client's own management team. Again, as Peter Prentice of Tyzack & Partners points out, there is always the chance that the chief executive of the client firm may also be a non-executive director of the firm from which a promising candidate has expressed interest in the vacancy. The headhunter is able to protect candidates from such awkward situations and also from the supreme gaffe (which happens all too often) of applying for their own jobs.

Nor should the headhunter's claim to bring expertise and objectivity to an assignment be airily dismissed as so much sales rhetoric. Knowing where to start and how to follow through are vital elements in any search or high-level selection assignment, and may well be a task beyond the powers and experience of even a large company. This part of the case was very well pleaded by Nigel Rugman of Management Appointments Ltd. in an article in the July 1981 edition of *The Director*:

"There is no such thing as a "standard" job or man specification for a senior executive role," he wrote. "Start
by defining the company's peculiar problems and opportunities in the marketplace and then analyse how these
impinge practically and politically upon the person to
be recruited. Similarly identify the personality type most
likely to prosper in the company's existing management
environment. Objectivity is the keynote of this process."

Obviously, a headhunter of integrity and perception is
better equipped to carry out this task than any "insider",
if only because he is not labouring in the corporate vineyard
but looking at the whole activity from an outside vantage
point. Or, to quote A.E. Young of Alexander Hughes &
Associates (U.K.) Ltd:

"A headhunter of experience who knows his job starts
with four advantages. He can help appriase the job and
assess the people the new man will have to work with,
from an independent viewpoint; he has long experience
in this specialist field and so has learnt appraisal techniques
as a result of his work, he has built up a network of
contacts and often a vast index of people; and he can
act as a confidential intermediary between the company
and the man, both of whom in the early stages might
want to retain their anonymity."

As already noted, however, one or two search consultancies do not favour keeping files or indices of people,
preferring to start afresh on every assignment. Leaving
aside any arguments as to which is the better approach, it
should be pointed out that the "no records" consultancy,
as in the case of his computerized competitor, must nevertheless have special skill and experience in knowing where
to start. Indeed, this skill plus the confidential nature of
the service could be said to make up most of the *raison
d'être* for search consultants: selection men, by contrast,
rely heavily on advertising skills and in sorting out sheep

from goats where large numbers are concerned.

A.E. Young refers also to the headhunter's skill in appraisal techniques, but it is worth emphasizing that, with most of the tribe, this is a skill acquired by experience and rarely fortified by formal training. This aspect of the headhunting art is looked at in greater detail in the next chapter. As with the overwhelming majority of recruiters within companies, however, the external recruiters rely primarily on the interview plus personal judgement in the construction of short-lists. As one consultant told me, "Recruitment consultancy is not about novel techniques, it is about the competence with which the standard methodology is employed". This is true as far as it goes, but there is no reason why the personnel department should not be able to apply the "standard methodology" just as well as the search or selection man, so the external consultant must be offering some additional service in order to survive, let alone prosper.

I have suggested that this additional service lies mainly in knowing where to start and in maintaining confidentiality, as far as search consultancies are concerned, and with selection firms in the writing and placing of effective advertisements and in sorting out the most likely applicants from large numbers. This is not to ignore the useful work which can be done by both branches of the trade, so to speak, in drawing up a good job profile in association with the client and in advising the latter on pay and perks for the post. Firms which choose to do their own recruiting for senior executive posts often tend to offer too little in return for too much, and as a result may waste not only a lot of managerial time but also considerable sums in fruitless advertising.

Again, two further, very useful skills the outside recruiter ought to be able to offer is the ability to arouse and retain the interest of the right people in the job in question and, equally important, to discourage without antagonising those applicants or candidates who, in his opinion, are not suitable. "The task of switching off a candidate, especially if his personality isn't right, is never an easy one", commented

George Harris of Canny Bowen, and his colleagues in the profession will utter a heartfelt "Amen" to that observation. The other skill referred to is that of acting as an intermediary in the final negotiating stages, on which one consultant claimed, somewhat paternalistically, that "to leave the client unaided at this point would be tantamount to incompetence". I stress the element of paternalism, yet there is no doubt that a strong streak of this runs the whole course of a typical search or selection assignment.

Other comments on this aspect of an assignment reveal a variation of emphasis while underlining that satifactory completion is very much a concern for most headhunters. If this is primarily because future business may be at stake, then it serves only to underline that professional recruitment is a commercial enterprise like any other. Anyhow, here are the views of some leading consultancies on rounding off assignments:-

"We always present our candidates personally and remain during the first meeting with the client. Thereafter we are at the disposal of both sides to give independent advice or assistance, but the final decision is always taken by the client and the candidate."

"It depends on the type of job. With selection, we get involved in reference checking, and the tendency today is to recommend. With search, we often process one candidate at a time the whole way."

"We hold the client's hand well past the shortlist stage; in fact, up to the appointment we make ourselves available to him for the discussion of and advice on candidates in the light of his interviews. We often also check after the candidate has started his/her job to make sure that all is going well."

"The client makes the final decision, but we ensure that he is aware of the pluses and minuses of his choice."

"We act to the point of a candidate's effective operation with his new company. We have no forms to complete of any significance and we reckon to be judged on performance after 18 months to two years."

I have tried to be as fair as possible to headhunters in these preceding pages because of the commonly held but frequently unjustifiable belief that they charge outrageous fees even when they fail to find a suitable candidate. Their placement rate, it is true, is by no means 100 per cent — 70 per cent is a good average — though of course it is much better to leave a key post unfilled than to appoint the wrong person. Let me just therefore round off the case for the defence by quoting Nigel Rugman of Management Appointments Ltd again:

"What the headhunter is selling is often intangible, and the client is paying very tangible money for it. He is in fact buying the individual headhunter's perception, experience and sensitivity as well as his time and effort."

Clients may not always see it this way, but the point deserves to be made.

Leaving aside for the moment the question of whether the recruitment industry offers value for money, it has to be said that the potential for profit within the industry is very good. Individual consultants in a successful search or selection business in a capital city should be able to generate at least £50,000 worth of business per year, while a few may bring in turnover worth double that figure. The Consultex SA survey of headhunting in Western Europe covering the year 1979 estimated, for example, that the search and recruitment markets in the U.K., West Germany, France, Belgium, Switzerland and the Netherlands earned an aggregate fee income (in U.S. dollars) of $102 million from a total of 6,710 assignments, with $70 million of this total coming from the first three countries. This works out roughly at $15,250 per assignment, and it should be borne in mind that the figures cover all forms of executive recruitment, and not simply the more expensive search assignments. "Fees charged for a search assignment", the survey claimed, "typically exceed $15,000 and often top several hundred thousand dollars." This latter claim, it must be admitted, sounds rather high, but it may apply to assignments involving the recruitment of perhaps two, three or more top executives for the same client. Anyhow the survey also came to the conclusion that headhunting was among the fastest growing and most lucrative areas of consulting.

It is a view endorsed by Eurosurvey Ltd, a leading consultancy in the EEC area, which also adds, in a special report on *Management Trends during 1980*, that "the vast majority of our assignments for industry are for line management. There is but little demand for appointments which are aimed at bringing in intellectual contributions to the company. Staff appointments — such as corporate planning — are very much at a discount and are even considered as a luxury." However, Eurosurvey also noted that service industries, such as banking, insurance, leisure and consulting itself, were maintaining a high demand for executive talent.

It would seem, then, come rain or shine, there is always a demand for the headhunter's services.

As noted in Chapter One, there are two basic options open to the organisation seeking to recruit from outside for a senior post — namely, selection or search — and although the approach differs, I see these as two parts of a whole known as "headhunting". "In both cases", Nigel Rugman points out, "you retain the consultant's services, but with selection the total fee ranges between 18-25 per cent of salary, plus the cost of advertising: with the latter, it is 30-35 per cent of salary, plus expenses. As a general rule, the advertising (selection) method is appropriate to appointments ranging in salary £10,000-£25,000 p.a. while search comes into play above this ceiling and when an appointment is exceptionally specialised."

These figures serve as a rough but useful guide, though some headhunters would quibble over the implication that most search men would be unlikely to handle any appointment salaried at less than £25,000 a year. I myself spoke to several whose lower limit was in the region of £15,000 a year, while among the specialist firms the "floor" can go down to £8,000 a year or even less. Again, although "percentage of salary" is the most common foundation on which headhunters base their fees, it is by no means the only method. Essentially, there are five basic methods as follows:-

1. Percentage of the annual salary of the appointment in question. This may range between 25-35 per cent, and in special cases up to 40 per cent. In the United Kingdom, 25-30 per cent is more usual, but it tends to be higher in Western Europe.

2. Daily rate. Some headhunter firms prefer to quote a daily rate – anything between £300 to £450 – on the grounds that the total fee will more accurately reflect the time spent on the assignment.

3. Fixed charge. Some search consultancies "taste" the job as a first step, then estimate the degree of difficulty and the time likely to take. An overall fee is then agreed in advance with the client.

4. Payment by results or contingency fees. Some firms offer their services on a "No placement, no fee" basis, a practice which is often condemned by the high priests of the search industry who allege this to be one of the marks of the "cowboy" headhunter – or perhaps "bounty hunter" is a more accurate description in their view. Their main argument against contingency fees is that the headhunter gives priority to "finding a body" rather than to meeting the true needs of the client. Be that as it may, according to the Consultex SA survey, payment by results is a growing trend in Western Europe.

5. The mixed approach. Quite a number of headhunter firms base their charges on a mix of the first three methods

described above. They argue that each assignment has its own individual character and problems, therefore an empiric approach — horses for courses — makes good sense.

As a footnote to all this, it ought to be pointed out that, with a contingency fee arrangement, the client firm is in no danger if it has the courage to say "No" until or unless it is presented with some candidate whom it really wants. If a headhunting firm chooses to go on presenting second raters, that is its own concern; the client is under no obligation to accept any of them. This perhaps explains why the practice seems to be finding favour in Europe, where industry does not have a tender heart. The great advantage to the client, of course, is that he knows he will not face a bill of several thousand pounds with no one to fill the vacant chair at the end of the day.

Such a situation can arise under the percentage of salary arrangement, although, to be fair, it happens only rarely. Much more often than not, the headhunter finds his man, even though the client may have been hoping secretly for someone a little better for his money. The fee, moreover, will certainly not be trifling. Simple arithmetic shows that at, say, 30% of £35,000 a year, the headhunter will receive £10,500 for perhaps a few weeks' hard work — or, if he charges a fixed fee, perhaps for a few days hard work. In such a situation the client really would be paying for the headhunter's "experience, perception and sensitivity", but the decision is up to himself and there is no reason why he should not shop around the recruitment industry for the best bargain. A search or selection consultancy with nothing to hide will not object to a potential customer making enquiries or taking up references.

Occasionally, of course, an organisation has no choice but to use a headhunter, for example, in a situation where it knows whom it wants but for "political" reasons cannot approach the individual in question directly. Quite a number of executive search assignments are of this "softly, softly" nature.

VALUE FOR MONEY?

Some comments from headhunters themselves on fees charged and the whole question of value for money make illuminating reading. Most of the firms quoted are leading consultancies in London and abroad.

"We act only at £20,000 a year plus. We put up a short-list of three candidates, but what does happen occasionally is that the client doesn't get the man he wants but he won't look at Nos. 2 and 3 on the list."

"We charge a fee based on the level of the appointment filled. Occasionally we work on a daily rate. The only expenses we charge are candidate/consultant travel, quoted in advance where overseas travel is involved. There can be no comparison with what it might cost a personnel department because it is just as different as using a Q.C. instead of a solicitor. Our minimum salary for a search job is £16,000 p.a. There are disadvantages to searching for appointments below that level, but we can and have done it at a fixed fee to assist a client."

"Our fees are based on our assessment of consulting time involved, and are usually quoted over a three-, four- or five-month period. They are thus based on our assessment of the number of days necessary to solve the client's problem. We have found in fact our fees are relatively more for lower paid posts and might even be cheaper than those of some competing firms for higher paid positions. This is because the amount of work to be done does not vary directly with the salary. Moreover, since we do not charge on a percentage of salary basis, there is no minimum salary level of appointment at which we will advise. However, since our minimum fee is £10,000, I doubt if many companies/clients would consider employing us for salaries of less than five figures. I have no idea of how our charges compare with those of recruiting through a personnel department."

"We normally charge a percentage of total remuneration; however, if the circumstances merit, we sometimes work on a daily rate. Direct cost comparisons with in-house personnel departments are not valid since one is not necessarily assuming equal results. The bulk of the appointments we are concerned with fall within the broad parameters of £10,000-£25,000 a year, with a bias towards the upper end. Where we feel that our services are not necessarily the most cost effective for the prospective client, we will say so, since this is in both our and the client's interest."

"Our fees are based on time expended and are marginally higher than the competition's. In practice, the minimum level of salary at which we act is £25,000 p.a., but actually depends upon the importance of the appointment in terms of direction of the business. Recruiting through the personnel department can be more economical for clear cut, low level jobs, but not where the profit to the enterprise as a whole is involved."

The above comments are, as I say, illuminating. They suggest a mixture of business sense, flexibility and a touch of arrogance or pomposity — qualities, in fact, one would expect to find in any group of managers. I am surprised, however, to find that the recruitment industry, especially the leading consultancies, seem to have made little or no attempt to compare their costs with those of personnel departments, even allowing for the fact that headhunters tend to concentrate on top-level appointments. Above all, the comments strongly underline the wisdom of shopping around in this market.

The time taken to complete an assignment is another vital element not only as regards cost but also as regards (often) the quality of the placement. As with many other aspects of living — a love affair or a house purchase, for instance — delays and frustrations often spell ruin for the whole venture, and in fact most professional recruiters derive a great deal of pleasure and satisfaction from completing an assignment both efficiently and quickly. Here is Nigel Rugman's view:

"The tight scheduling of each stage is an essential factor in achieving success. The fewer the delays and the greater the sense of urgency, the more likely you are to be successful (always assuming of course that thoroughness is not compromised). Measuring a recruitment process in weeks rather than in months is the sure way of ensuring that no one goes off the boil."

Nor, to quote Dr Samuel Johnson, is it any "cynical aspersion" to point out the more swiftly assignments are successfully completed, the higher the turnover and profit of the consultancy concerned.

Yet the proof of this particular pudding is, as it were, in the hiring. Headhunters are rarely retained because they are cheap but because they may well be the cheapest and most effective means of finding the man an organisation wants and needs. The truth of the matter is that most enterprises just do not know where and how to start on the task of finding people with the right skills and track record to fill key positions.

This truth is reflected in particular by the figures for the search industry in the U.S.A. There, between 1977 and 1980, it is estimated that the average total revenue growth among the six leading search consultancies (the "Big Six", as they are called; Korn/Ferry, Heidrick & Struggles, Russell Reynolds, Spencer Stuart, Boyden Associates, Egon Zehnder) leapt by an astonishing 110 per cent to $120.9 million; even though they do not allow for inflation, these are impressive figures. At the same time, revenues of the sixty-plus members of the (American) Association of Executive Recruiting Consultants saw their revenues increase by an average of 74%, to a total billing of $100 million a year. However, according to the publication, *Executive Recruiter News*, the total turnover for the external recruitment industry in the U.S.A. is in the region of $1 billion.

Whatever one may say of individual headhunting firms,

however costly and unrewarding an individual client's experience at the hands of the industry, statistics like these add up to a formidably powerful case for the services they offer. As Peter Prentice of Tyzack & Partners observed, "Forget about the cowboys. They have been largely found out and driven out by the competition in the marketplace. The proof of a consultancy's integrity is largely bound up in the fact that it survives and prospers."

True enough, but there is one important qualification. It is to be found in a practice which continues to disillusion many existing clients and to frighten off many would-be clients, and serves to tarnish, fairly or unfairly, the image of the search industry as a whole. It is of course the accusation of "poaching", which forms the subject of the next chapter.

Finally, most headhunters would point out, and with justification, that recruiting costs become largely irrelevant if these lead to a dramatic increase in a company's profitability or, in these hard times make all the difference between closure and survival. George Harris of Canny Bowen Associates, for instance, tells the story of how some 14 years ago his consultancy acted for a company with a £50 million turnover. "Today", he added, "turnover has risen to £500 million and there are only two people on the main board whom we haven't placed."

6

Poacher or Honest Broker?

The most common accusation launched at headhunters —
and not only by their enemies — is that of "poacher", and
the cardinal sin of the industry is more or less unanimously
thought to be that of poaching from a client — that is,
"searching" someone from a client firm and enticing him to
accept another appointment. When the person so enticed
was in fact placed in his existing job only a short time previously by the headhunter in question, then that is often
regarded as a sin for which there is no forgiveness.

Many headhunters will cheerfully and honestly admit to
"poaching" in the ordinary sense of persuading some talented
executive to leave firm A for firm B. "Why deny the charge,"
commented George Harris, "because that is what we do.
However, we never poach from our own clients, and remember that in any case we are dealing with mature and able
people who are perfectly capable of making up their own
minds. I also happen to believe that every job has a life cycle."

Another headhunter, David Blamey, claims that companies
expect their best men to be "searched" these days. "One
chief executive", he added, "actually told me that 'it keeps
us on our toes'!" This ties in with Garry Long's observation
that confidentiality is not always as important as suggested
because few employers expect high flyers to stay indefinitely in the one job.

"Look at it this way", commented Bert Young. "Really top men don't spend their time looking at job advertisements. In fact, the wife of one senior executive who was going places said to me: 'You're my husband's insurance policy'."

(The view that top executives are rarely to be found poring over the job columns is not universally shared among the headhunters, but it is of little importance.)

While the above arguments are persuasive if not actually seductive, it must be added that industry does not generally see the case for poaching in this light; in fact, companies have an understandable resentment against good executives being enticed away — as often as not to rival firms — even though such moves can often loosen a career log-jam in the "victim" organisation. Typical comments in the BIM/IPM survey included:

"The disadvantage of executive search consultants is that they cause movement — some of the more disreputable ones place people and then in a year or so ring them up with another vacancy."

"I would be frightened if I got someone from the headhunters that six months or a year later they would be approached by the same people."

These are understandable fears backed by much hard evidence. Executive talent is in limited supply, especially in the case of sharply profiled appointments, so the none too scrupulous headhunter is sometimes unable to resist the temptation of using his best material over and over again, as it were. Even the more reputable consultancies are beginning to think and act in terms of imposing a time limit on their "self restraint", with two years being regarded as a decent interval. On the other hand, most headhunters feel no need for any restraint whatsoever in cases where people whom they have placed become restless and in turn approach them with a view to changing jobs. Again, it must be said, that it is not always the headhunter who does the enticing in the first place. As Bert Young makes clear, the headhunter, in his peregrinations throughout industry, gets to know a lot of people and gets "a constant stream of willing victims letting it coyly be known they might be open to offers."

Yet when all's said and done, poaching is very much a fact of headhunting life, to put it at its most banal, so why it should be thought of as singularly pernicious is something of a mystery. Compared with some transfer deals involving soccer stars, the practice verges on the realms of innocence. The reason is perhaps that the "transferred executive" invariably proves a great deal more valuable to the business which hires him than does the soccer star to his new club. And of course a lot less expensive!

Nevertheless, if the recruitment profession in the United Kingdom wishes to prove that today it is both more respectable and a lot more professional, it cannot rely merely on success in the marketplace to make its point. That may be enough for the practitioners themselves, but to clients and others it has to demonstrate that it has standards and lives up to them. In theory, there is an Association of Executive Search Consultants but, in the words of one headhunter, "it is not a very active body"; that, indeed, almost qualifies as the understatement of the year. What the profession urgently needs is its own watchdog cum public relations executive body, which can at one and the same time establish a code of practice and defend the aims and activities of the profession. Priority number one for any such body must be to bring members together to agree a set of rules governing the "poaching" of their own clients' executives. The fact that these executives may be approached by other headhunting firms is irrelevant; self-regulation, as in other realms of business and management, must always remain the basis of any real standards.

Such a challenge, be it noted, is already being faced up to by the much more active Association of Executive Recruiting Consultants (A.E.R.C.) in the U.S.A., whose 62 members include the leading search and selection firms in that country. Confronted with what they believe to be a chronic shortage

of top executive talent, on the one hand, and client resentment at poaching on the other, the Association's members
are trying to develop a flexible procedure as regards what
are known on the other side of the Atlantic as "off limits
agreements". According to Herbert E. Meyer, in an article
in *Fortune* in September 1981, "Off-limits agreements have
come to depend on how far the search firms think a particular client can be pushed."

Some clients, according to Meyer, will not budge at all
on the off-limits rule, and one of them — Jim Curvey, vice-
president and director of personnel at Chase Manhattan
Bank — was reported as saying, "If you do business with us,
the client is the entire bank", implying that headhunters
should not consider a separate division of the Bank to be a
separate business.

The Big Six, Meyer continued, have been insisting that
the off-limits rule must be softened not merely that they
can keep on growing but to save them from shrinking,
because "too many client companies had begun to take
unfair advantage of the rule by hiring each of the Big Six
firms one every two years to fill a relatively low-paid (and
low-fee) position in order to keep everybody in the company
off limits indefinitely."

Various solutions to this impasse are being talked about.
One is that clients agree to provide headhunters with a
minimum amount of business or number of searches over a
given period. Another suggestion is that headhunters "go
vertical", encouraging clients to use headhunters to recruit
not only top executives but others lower down the ladder,
and in subsidiary companies as well as at headquarters.
Other headhunters simply argue for greater flexibility in
the approach to the problem. The point is, however, that
the most powerful firms in the U.S. headhunting industry
are thinking about the problem and seeking solutions, and
some of the proposals suggest that the leading figures in
the industry are very powerful indeed. Who would have
thought a few years ago, for example, that any headhunter
would ever be in a position to require that a client firm give

him a minimum amount of business in any year to protect his best men from any outside offers? In any case, such protection is in the nature of things always strictly limited, for there is nothing to prevent their being approached by any other outside recruiter.

As far as the really big organisations are concerned, the answer may well lie in going vertical, because in any event there is a powerful case for the headhunter/client relationship to develop to the point at which the headhunter in fact becomes an executive manpower adviser to the client, perhaps acting for him on some retainer basis. Over a period such an arrangement is bound to result in advantages to both parties, as the headhunter gets to know his client's needs and problems more and more intimately and is able to offer what in effect is a combination of a recruitment and executive development service involved, among other activities, in planning for the management succession — that most neglected of all senior management functions. This, as I see it, will be the next major advance within the search industry at the top end of the market.

Yet the business of "poaching" is one which must be resolved if headhunting is to achieve the reputation it would wish for itself. One leading headhunter with pronounced views on the folly of poaching off a client is Christopher Wysock Wright, chief executive of Wrightson Wood, a well known executive search firm in Knightsbridge, SW1. "The need to maintain a rigid code regarding client companies as off-limits is a number one priority", he stresses. "Certainly this is sometimes broken, but it remains a vital safeguard from the point of view of the client. For the search consultant, there may be short-term gains to be had by abandoning the code, but such action is also short-sighted."

Christopher Wysock Wright also argues, rightly, that if the business of search is to be taken seriously, "our corporate clients must relay on standards of behaviour which they would expect from other professional services."

"Apart from any other considerations", he points out, "search often spills over into more general counselling in human resources terms for client firms and this necessarily means an overall commitment to the client's well-being and internal culture. Our success depends on the development of mutual trust, particularly as we operate in a highly sensitive area of management."

Even so, it looks as if poaching will go on as long as headhunting itself exists, for the essence of the activity is that the search men must induce men of proven ability to leave one job for another, and the most which can be expected is that headhunters will regard their own clients as off-limits.

In itself, moreover, given that this constraint is observed, "poaching" can scarcely be regarded as unethical; most certainly it is not a cardinal commercial sin. In a free society, people are at liberty to change their jobs and to sell their talents and experience to the highest bidder, even though it can also be fairly claimed that in most countries the bias of employment legislation since World War II has been running strongly against the employer. Self-regulation within the recruitment industry itself can do much to control the worst abuses and to keep the legislators at bay, apart from which it is in the industry's own commercial interest to be seen to be bound by an ethical code of its own devising. At the time of writing, this code seems to operate in patches, and the "cowboys" can still make a living in what ought to be one of the most disciplined sectors of the whole business arena.

7
Government takes a Hand

The notion that government may one day become a major headhunter in its own right may strike many people as wildly improbable, even though one or two industries in the public sector are beginning to use independent headhunters. In the United Kingdom, the best known appointments via this route are of course those of Sir Michael Edwardes to British Leyland and Ian MacGregor to British Steel, while at the very peak of government, the Prime Minister, Margaret Thatcher, sought out Sir Derek Rayner of Marks & Spencer to direct a wind of change through Civil Service bureaucracy.

It may be fanciful to see these appointments as initial steps towards the creation of an official headhunting team charged with finding top talent to direct and administer the process of government, though I have no doubt that such a development would be warmly welcomed among recruiters and no doubt among the public at large; after all, nothing could more emphatically set a seal of respectability on the headhunting industry, and who knows how often such a team might call on independent headhunters for assistance. Fantasy this may well be for the time being, but already one or two headhunters are beginning to claim that official use of their services is growing — slowly but steadily. R.A.B. Gowlland of Egon Zehnder International was speaking for a large section of the industry when he told me that Government departments will make increasing use of the services of firms in the executive search field, though certainly if a Socialist government is elected, there will be increasing pressure towards more onerous licensing regulations. That, however, would not imply official hostility to the activity as such, merely to its being an entirely free market enterprise.

"There is in fact an approved list of headhunters for government", claims Christopher Wysock-Wright, "and the main users are the Departments of Industry, Trade and Defence. Today's civil servants understand the use of search but not so the politicians. No. 10 Downing Street would think you should be honoured to find someone for a top official post and that fees do not come into it."

Introducing PER
As things are, the Government of the day is actively involved in the headhunting process — and not just as a client — through the activities of the Professional and Executive Register (PER) which is a limb of the Department of Employment. Set up in June 1973, PER is, more precisely, a specialist arm of the Employment Service Division of the Manpower Services Commission, and is charged with two main tasks. First, it sets out in a variety of ways to help jobseekers in professional and managerial occupations in their job search, and its services are available without charge to employed and unemployed alike, being financed to a large extent by government grant. These services include any necessary advice or assessment, plus practical guidance on self-help, retraining, relocation and all public services available to the jobseeker.

PER's second task, it claims, follows naturally from the first. To obtain a continuing flow of vacancies at the level in which it operates — mostly middle and junior management — it offers a professional recruitment service to employers. In addition to maintaining a register of candidates, it organises advertising in the open market through the pages of its own weekly publication, *Executive Post*, and also screens and classifies candidates up to final shortlist stage. These latter are commercial functions, it points out, and are charged to employers on a commercially competitive basis.

It is seen, then, that PER belongs to the selection sector of the headhunting industry, where in fact, according to its director, Geoff Crosby, it is responsible for filling more than 15% of all personnel and executive vacancies on the open market in Britain.

"In the selection sector, we're far and away the biggest agency", Crosby told me. "Even so, our penetration is not so high as we would have hoped, either from a commercial or public service point of view."

PER does not in fact enjoy a high reputation among other recruitment agencies, which are all too ready to point out that it is currently operating at a loss, that it deals with the "lower end of the market" and that in any case its large market share can be explained primarily by its having a network of offices throughout the country and a staff of 500. "Staff has in fact been reduced from a peak of 800", Geoff Crosby pointed out, "but at the same time we've had to deal with 70% more jobseekers because of the recession."

The criticisms levelled against PER by the independents in the recruitment industry are valid up to a point but do not tell the whole story. It is too easily forgotten that it is a community service as well as a commercial undertaking, and, in the first of these roles, it faces commitments and restraints which are not found in the private sector. Chief of these commitments is that it is charged with helping the redundant executive, and this is a species whom most members of the independent recruitment industry — selection and search specialists alike — will have very little to do with. In this connection, Mr Tom Carew, head of Coutts Careers Counselling Ltd, makes the very pertinent point that "far too many recruiters forget, if they ever knew, that very often it is the job and not the man which is redundant."

Be that as it may, the constraint of having to provide a community service is bound to affect any official approach to the open recruitment market. Against this must be set the fact of support from public funds and the undoubted attraction behind the fact that its services are free to the redundant executive or professional man, so much so that by the late 1970s PER could claim to be filling one third of all executive vacancies handled by consultancies or agencies in this country. "Taking our overseas operations into account", says PER, "we are now the largest executive recruitment agency in the U.K." A brief look at how all this came about is well worthwhile, for it could point the way to the future role of government in this field.

Origins
State employment services began to operate in Britain in 1909 under the auspices of the Board of Trade, and in fact the first Labour Exchange in the country was opened by none other than (as he then was) Mr. Winston Churchill. The term "Employment Exchange" was officially adopted when the Ministry of Labour was created in 1917. As one would expect, these exchanges dealt at first almost exclusively with manual and clerical wage-earners who formed the vast bulk of the working population, and who were hardest hit by the high rate of unemployment during the harsh times of the 1920s and 1930s. In those years, the Labour Exchanges acquired an eleemosynary, flat cap, dole queue ethos which still hovers to some extent over the Job Centres of today's Department of Employment and may to some extent frustrate any attempt to project a government department as an efficient, sophisticated team serving the upper end of the recruitment market.

Anyway, in pre-war days, professionally qualified and managerial staff never appeared at an Employment Exchange, nor did it ever occur to employers to recruit for senior posts through the State system. A radical change emerged, however, at the end of the Second World War when many people of professional and executive standing, their careers disrupted by military service, could not easily resume where they left off. Others, who had been taken directly from school or university, hardly knew how to begin looking for a job when their service in the Forces ended. Therefore, to help individuals such as these, the then Ministry of Labour created a Technical and Scientific Register, which has become the Professional and Executive Register of today. In this, it ought to be added, government led the private recruitment sector by some ten years, for it was not until the mid-1950s that the independent executive recruitment consultancies really began to dominate the market led by Management Selection Ltd.

Whatever its shortcomings, the Technical and Scientific Register of those early post-war years had the sense to realise that a different approach would be needed if it was to serve the professional end of the employment spectrum. Candidates and employers alike would require highly individual handling while the recruitment staff themselves would have to possess knowledge and experience (and, preferably, qualifications) in the relevant area. Thirdly, a closer and more informal relationship with clients would have to be fostered, one which nevertheless retained a "proper distance" befitting any relationship between government and the public it purports to serve. In a word, the new service would have to develop an "identity" of its very own.

A charge to employers

From the beginning, the new Register adopted the practice of making no charge for its services either to employee or employer, and this continued until the overall review of public employment services of 1972. In that year the Department of Employment decided that the Professional and Executive Register had to continue its operations, as these, it was claimed, served some 2½ million people, or about 10% of the labour force. On the other hand, the service had to be extensively modernised, so it seemed reasonable that part of the cost should be borne by the employer users.

"The problem", states PER, "was boldly attacked by turning the Register into a composite organisation, part social service and part commercial venture. Under this revised brief, it was to maintain and develop the personal assistance given to individuals in professional and managerial occupations, with the identifiable costs of doing so being paid for directly from public funds."

"At the same time, the services offered to employers would be expanded to cover the entire range of modern recruiting methods, and this operation would be financed by making commercial charges and dynamised by competing in the market place with the established private agencies."

Computer matching of job and candidate was one of the modern recruiting methods favoured by PER over the first few years. In the middle of 1980, however, the Register effected a fundamental change by rejecting the computer in favour of a system of self-selection, or self-service, based on the job advertisements placed in *Executive Post* mainly by employers in both the public and private sectors and by overseas organisations.

According to Geoff Crosby, the commercial history of PER to date has fluctuated markedly. "Taking 1974-75 as our first trading year", he told me, "we operated at a loss for the first three years, then for the second three-year period we were in surplus, but since 1979-80 we have been operating at a loss because of the recession. Yet fee earnings have grown significantly over the period, from £2,364,000 in 1976-77 to £4,204,000 in 1979-80 and to an anticipated £5 million for 1981-82." The actual figures for 1976 to 1980 were as follows:-

	1976-77 £000s	1977-78 £000s	1978-79 £000s	1979-80 £000s
Commercial earnings	£2,364	£3,264	£3,860	£4,204
Social Activity Grants	£2,522	£2,761	£3,050	£3,520
Total income	£4,886	£6,025	£6,910	£7,730
Expenditure	£5,192	£5,925	£6,720	£7,627
Balance	-£306	+£100	+£190	+£103

PER, unfortunately, is unlikely to claim a surplus for 1981-82. "There will be an expenditure of £9 million plus", Geoff Crosby admitted, "and we hope to bring in about £5 million." Obviously the main reason for this considerable gap is to be found in the increasing amount of social activity – i.e. acting for the jobless – as a result of the recession.

A national network

The Professional and Executive Register is a separately managed part of the D.O.E's Employment service Division and as such is ultimately responsible to the Manpower Services Commission. It was designed as a nationwide service, with 38 offices in large towns throughout Great Britain, and these are now formally grouped into three geographical divisions – namely, Northern, Central and Southern. Each division in turn is sub-divided into areas to ensure (in impeccable officialese) "effective local management control and to facilitate inter-office cooperation." One regional office in each of the three major territories is nominated as "divisional office" to promote both cooperation and competition.

For their part, divisional offices are responsible directly to PER's head office in London, at 4-5 Grosvenor Place, SW1X 7SB. Headquarters also houses three specialist groups: PER Overseas, Executive Secretaries and Graduate Appointments.

Size undoubtedly accounts for the fact that PER can claim to fill some 16 per cent of all U.K. executive vacancies on the open market. It employs some 200 recruitment consultants, 300 candidate consultants and 24 training consultants backed up by support and management personnel throughout its network of offices. "Whilst avoiding expensive High Street sites", the service states, "it would be counter-productive to hide such facilities in dingy, back-street premises, so PER conforms with the competition in making use of attractive and accessible positions in commercial business areas."

This commercial approach is continued in the financing

of its services to employers, which are expected to pay for themselves through fee charges. Initially, PER lost money on these, but adds that "these losses steadily reduced as business expanded so that for the past three years 100% of costs have been recouped and a small operating profit achieved." By contrast, the community services of PER are not fee charging. Their identifiable costs include the expenses of advisory interviews, candidate seminars, administering the Employment Transfer Scheme, special training activities and the like, and these costs are met by government grant. Most of the expected loss of £4 million for 1981-82 undoubtedly derives from the fact that, since the recession, the Register has had to cope with a 70% increase in the number of job-seekers.

"Even so," Geoff Crosby commented, "our penetration has not been so high as we would have liked, either from a commercial or public service point of view. This is partly because there is no government tradition in the commercial recruitment sector and partly because the vast majority of executive vacancies are still filled through the traditional method of advertising."

And although he did not say so, the reason why the response from job-seekers has not been quite as great as expected is almost certainly linked with the fact that out of work executives still have greater faith in the independent consultancies, just as clerical and secretarial staff prefer the private employment agencies to the Job Centres.

Everyone of professional or executive standing is entitled to make use of PER's services in advancing his or her career, stresses its management somewhat piously. This applies whether the candidate is employed or unemployed or has had previous work experience or not. When enrolling, candidates are required to supply details of qualifications and job history. Once enrolled, they receive a weekly copy of *Executive Post* containing a continuous review of job and career opportunities in the form of advertisements backed by special articles, while from time to time PER also circulates details of candidates to suitable employers. Automatic checks are made at regular intervals as to whether or not candidates are still available.

On enrolment, each candidate is also sent a folder containing a booklet on job hunting, and it must be stressed that PER's services are available to those already in jobs but seeking a career change as well as to redundant and unemployed executives. The latter, however, may attend seminars for guidance in seeking and obtaining work, while candidates who lack skill in the jobs market are encouraged to take PER's three-day course in self-presentation. These demonstrate the techniques of self-assessment and of approaching employers in the most productive way through skilled letter writing, CV compilation and interviewing. Checks, claims PER, have shown that this effort is well justified by results.

"During 1980-81, Geoff Crosby said, "some 22,000 job-seekers attended our job-hunting courses, representing a 34% increase over the total for 1979-80, while our change to self-selection through *Executive Post* has proved much, much more acceptable to the job-seeker than computer marketing. Another statistic is that some 300,000 job-seekers enrolled with us during 1980-81 and, as I've already said, we were involved in finding candidates for more than 16,000 jobs of which our share of actual placements was 4,500."

PER's business face

"A complete and business-like recruitment service to industry, commerce and other employers with vacancies for executive, managerial, professional and semi-professional staff" is how PER describes what it regards as the business end of its operations. Assignments, it stresses, are handled personally by a recruitment consultant who is appointed to take sole responsibility for the recruiting exercise concerned, and he confers with the employer to obtain an accurate job description along with other details of the candidate preferred, such as age, qualifications, experience, salary range and so on. It is very much the same approach as with a private selection consultancy except that, in Crosby's own words, "being in a volume market we tend to deal more with junior and middle managers." The "independents" themselves make very little use of the Register's services and facilities, "but not", Grosby emphasises, "because we are unwilling. If requested, we will cheerfully search our candidate bank on behalf of a selection agency."

But to continue with the PER methodology. Details of vacancies are immediately prepared for the forthcoming edition of *Executive Post* (though occasionally they may be kept for a special supplement) and the replies are "refined" by the consultant to produce an accurate shortlist for the client. PER also makes arrangements for candidates to attend for interview, and can offer clients interviewing facilities on its own premises. Or, alternatively, PER will interview candidates on the client's behalf with a view to reducing the initial shortlist to two or three particularly suitable people. "This", it claims, "not only saves the employer's time but also ensures that the creaming is carried out by fully trained, professional interviewers."

The Professional & Executive Register, in addition, organises national or local advertising through its own PERad service, which allows firms of any size to use its advertising agency; it points out, moreover, that its composite advertisements offer clients the pulling power of a large display advertisement — currently, in fact, PER places more press advertising under its own name than does any other single recruitment agency, but of course the resources at the Register's disposal through government support funds has always to be borne in mind when assessing these comparisons. It also handles all response to advertising, replying to every approach and "integrating" (sic) the best candidates with the selection of those with whom it is already in contact.

The three "special services" of PER are as follows:

1. *PER Overseas.* This recruits in Great Britain for any foreign-based company seeking British personnel for employment overseas. Here, perhaps, is a good point at which

to stress that the somewhat tarnished reputation from which British management sometimes suffers in its own country does not apply overseas. British managers are highly thought of in Europe, and the Middle and Far East especially. The service also recruits for British companies needing local nationals.

2. *Executive Secretaries*. This operates from London and Birmingham, and concentrates on the market for personal assistants and highly qualified secretaries.

3. *Graduate Appointments*. This service deals specifically with new graduates from colleges and polytechnics and with school leavers, and works closely with university appointments boards and like bodies (of which more in the next chapter).

PER charges for its services to employer clients on what it describes as "a commercially competitive basis" and it emphasizes that 30% of the job-seekers with whom it deals are already employed. "Of course", Crosby added, "we don't know how many of them are under threat but then neither does any other selection agency. We're brokers in the middle and we can't affect the supply and demand position, but only the public sector can provide the information and support services which is all a lot of job-seekers at executive level really need."

Like those of any other business, PER's charges are of necessity linked to its costs and overheads, but in 1981 it was charging clients £175 per advertisement insertion of 150-175 words in *Executive Post*, and £225 with a confidential reply service thrown in. It also charges a placement fee based on a percentage of annual salary, just like any other selection consultancy — "If, that is, they want selection", Crosby made clear.

Another significant fact about PER's pattern of business is that government departments and firms in the public sectors make proportionately less use of its services than those in the private sector. The reason, according to Crosby, is that most public sector industries have their own personnel departments and do not buy in selection services

91

(though, as already noted, they are beginning to buy in search services). As to clients from the private sector, PER says that they reflect a typical spread from industry and commerce.

A justification

This profile of a government-supported selection consultancy operating in both the public and private sectors prompts much interesting speculation. For example, will PER flourish during the 1980s and perhaps add executive search to its list of activities, or will it fall victim one day to a Chancellor with a sharp axe. Although it is currently costing the taxpayer money, the latter fate would seem quite undeserved. Apart from the fact of 4,500 placements a year, the head-hunting jungle ought to have one or two clearings in which refuge centres can be set up for the putative and the not so successful executives. The young graduate or A-levels man who has not yet got a foot in the door, and the executive who has lost his job, often for reasons other than incompetence, need a helping hand. This is not to imply criticism of the people at the top end of the search industry who deal only with the talented, the experienced and the successful — they have their living to make — but the recruitment profession as a whole must cast a wider net and be seen to do so.

Meanwhile, it has to be admitted that PER does not seem to cut a great deal of ice among the middle and upper reaches of the recruitment industry. According to the BIM/IPM 1980 survey on *Selecting Managers*, "this source is not widely used, only 23% of companies (i.e. respondents) using it more than occasionally."

The report goes on to comment that, among patrons of PER, there is little variation by company size, although those with over 5,000 employees tend to make less use of the service. In fact, it adds, the extent of use reflects more the job function and seniority of the post than any geographical or industry sector patterns. "PER is generally viewed", says the survey, "as being most appropriate for scientific, technical and engineering posts. It is considered unsuitable for senior management posts, and respondents indicated that its use is mainly confined to appointments at graduate and junior management levels."

Almost by way of a footnote, it is worth adding that scientific and engineering vacancies have now "infiltrated" the upper regions of the executive search territory, reflecting the increasing demand among companies for people with proven records and qualifications, for doers rather than planners.

The 64,000-dollar question, however, is surely: Does PER's operating experience to date make it any more or less likely that Government will one day take an active part in executive search?

Such a development, as stated, would no doubt help to polish the professional image of headhunters. On the other hand, it might seriously cut into the headhunters' market even if such a government task force confined its activities to searching for civil service departments and nationalised industries, for these areas over the next decade are likely to yield rich pickings for the search industry. It has to be asked, moreover, whether there would be any point in Government creating such a team when, as things are, the existing recruitment industry is perfectly capable of doing the job. More capable, in fact, for government employees in the nature of things would be under much greater constraints and restrictions than private headhunters. Inevitably, as public servants, all manner of "policy" considerations would inhibit them from, say, raiding the managerial resources of a supplier organisation or those of one public industry to nourish another. The spectre of "Questions in the House" looms large over the whole idea. In short, it is much better to hire a private consultancy to do one's dirty work if it is Government which is buying.

PER, obviously, faces many problems and has still a lot to learn, but something along the lines of its present remit seems to be its most suitable role. Competing in the marketplace through its service to employers helps it provide a more efficient service in its social role.

8

The Milk Round

Helping hands for graduates

Mention in the previous chapter of PER's Graduate Appointments Service focuses attention on an area of headhunting which, although concerned with people who are still wet behind the ears as far as managerial experience is concerned, is in the long run every bit as important as the search activities going on in more exalted circles. I refer of course to the annual prospecting by personnel departments among our universities (and, to some degree, among polytechnics) in quest of tomorrow's executives, professional and scientific staff. For some reason, this activity is known in the trade as "The Milk Round", which happens to reflect — no doubt unintentionally — the fact that cream floats to the top. It is, frankly, an exercise in elitism, and none the worse for that.

Any account of the working of The Milk Round inevitably bogs writer and reader down in a world of initials, so it is best to get these over and done with right away. At "official" level, there are three main bodies underpinning this recruitment carousel — namely:-

The Association of Graduate Careers Advisory Services (AGCAS);
The Standing Conference of Employers of Graduates (SCOEG); and

The Central Services Unit (CSU), which provides administrative and information services for AGCAS and is based
at Manchester University.

If we add PER's Graduates Appointment Service — and why
not? then The Milk Round can claim to be supported by a
very helpful quartet.

As its name implies, SCOEG is the organisation for companies who recruit graduates on a regular and substantial
basis. It claims to have a growing membership (more than
400 at the end of 1980) and to represent many small employers as well as large, well known companies. Be that as it
may, and in spite of an upsurge in private sector graduate
recruitment since the second world war, companies employing fewer than 200 staff account for only 15 per cent of all
graduate vacancies even though in terms of numbers they
form an almost overwhelming majority of businesses. It is
a classic example of Pareto's Law. SCOEG members in fact
recruit more than 80 per cent of graduates entering the
private sector, and a feature of its work is a Code of Practice
for the recruitment of graduates agreed with the National
Union of Students.

Graduate careers advisory services, of which AGCAS is
the spearhead, have expanded dramatically over the past
ten years to keep up with the continuous growth in student
numbers. In 1980, for example, a total of 86,664 students
graduated from universities (first and higher degrees) and
polytechnics (first degrees only) in the United Kingdom,
and an increase of 5 per cent was expected for 1981.

Another reason for the expansion of these advisory services, claims PER, is that the nature of graduate recruitment has changed. It has expanded because "competition
for recruits in certain fields has increased, as job requirements become ever more complex", while on the students'
side there is growing anxiety over unemployment, especially
in areas where demand is low.

"There is a tendency for students to accept unsuitable
jobs", said Brian Putt, director of the Central Services Unit

(CSU), "because they panic, and there seems to be more reneging on offers by both employers and candidates. With increasing sophistication of both application procedures and the work available, student counselling is more important than ever."

Brian Putt also gave me a break-down of the 1980 graduate employment figures for the United Kingdom. Schopenhauer, that most readable of all philosophers, once described journalism as "the second hand on the watch of history" and, by extension, a year's statistics perhaps can be seen to represent the minute hand. In this case, however, the figures can be taken as representative of a much longer period and to be typical of the times.

Where they went

Of the 86,664 who graduated from British universities in 1980, then, 67,368 students took a first degree, and of them 29,597 were known to have taken up permanent employment by July 1981. Of these, 7,413 took up posts in manufacturing, 1,174 in building, 1,311 in public utilities, 3,203 in engineering research and development, 2,618 in administration, operative management and production, 1,766 in scientific research and development, 1,294 in civil and environmental planning, 787 in scientific and engineering support services, 1,953 in marketing and buying, 2,129 in management services (including computing), 400 into the legal profession, while the information and library services claimed 649 graduates. Manufacturing apart, comparatively large numbers were also attracted into financial services (5,057) and personnel and welfare work (6,857), while (significantly) teaching and lecturing could accommodate only 983 graduates. The remainder took up various occupations.

Of the 19,296 students taking higher degrees, only 4,888 were known to have entered permanent employment, and of these 1,140 went into manufacturing industries, 130 went into building and 214 into public utilities. What happened to the remainder of the first and higher degree graduates can only be guessed at, but no doubt some went on to study for higher degrees, others may have emigrated or obtained posts abroad and some, of course, probably had to go on the dole. The recession does not always take note of educational attainments.

At this point it is worth mentioning the work of PER's Graduate Appointments Service, which is used mostly by students without firm offers of employment by the end of their final term. In fact, all graduates who sign on as unemployed are automatically registered with PER, which, among other things, produces literature designed specifically for graduates seeking their first job. Their position on the Register is reviewed after 13 weeks, when those who are still without a job are given a more comprehensive information pack — which reminds one somewhat of the parson in Oscar Wilde's *Ballad of Reading Gaol* who called every day and "left a little tract".

The sad aspect of all this, according to Dorothy Cooke, PER's graduate appointment manager, "is that some graduates are still looking for a suitable job a year after graduation, and at this stage we have to advise them to apply for lower grade jobs so that they can get the work experience they so desperately need. Once they are in work, their chances of moving in to a position more suitable for graduates are greatly improved."

To return, however, to the work of AGCAS. According to Kenneth Dibden, who was chairman of the Association from 1977 to 1979 and who is now director of the University of London Careers Advisory Service, "these services are making a determined effort to reach all students well before the final year to encourage them to look at career choices and look at the direction they want to take before graduation. In the final year, students are then encouraged to talk with careers officers, while many careers advisory services offer seminars on job application procedures and interview techniques."

The actual administration of graduate recruitment, as stated, is in the hands of the CSU, which centralises the information functions of the Careers Advisory Services. A feature of this work is the production of a fortnightly bulletin entitled *Current Vacancies*, which circulates through the universities and offers advertising at low cost to the employer. PER, too, uses this publication from time to time to advertise vacancies on its books.

No practical alternative
Anyhow, there is general agreement among the three sets of initials, as it were, i.e. SCOEG, AGCAS and CSU, that the Milk Round is the best mechanism for dealing with the challenge of giving graduates a start in business life — and it would indeed be surprising if they did not agree on this. According to Kenneth Dibden:

"No one's come up with a better way, and a lot of people have tried. By seeing a lot of candidates at an early stage and by giving wide exposure to the organisation and the vacancies it is offering, the employer has the greatest chance of attracting and ultimately recruiting graduates of high calibre."

This view must carry a good deal of conviction at the present time when four out of every five vacancies for graduates are contained within the private sector — an encouraging trend in itself — and when two out of every five of these are in manufacturing industry. Moreover, graduates are now commanding a greater proportion of available jobs as work becomes increasingly complex while the expansion of higher and further education has lowered the number of able people leaving school and going straight into employment.

View from the other side
But what about the view of the Milk Round from the other side? I discussed this with Kenneth Woodward of MSL's Birmingham office who used to be a member of the Courtauld team which visits certain universities each year on a talent-spotting tour.

"The careers advisory service at each university is the

focal point between the company and the student", he stressed. "In our own case we would send literature about the company and the prospects it offered in the September prior to the start of the students' final year, then in the November we would do a small, informal presentation. We would interview students who expressed interest during the second term when we carried out a programme of visits; at some universities we would see any students, at others only technical students, for two-thirds of our intake was technical. During the Easter vacation a second series of interviews would be held at our own premises. All in all, we'd get about 2,000 applications and interview about 700 the first time round. Some 300 to 400 would be given a second interview, of whom about 150 would receive job offers. Acceptances would number between 70 and 80."

Because of the nature of the employment being offered by Courtauld's, the search effort was concentrated on certain universities with a good technical reputation and which the company favoured partly because of the quality of the previous intake. These universities included Birmingham, Bristol, Cambridge, Edinburgh, Glasgow, Leeds, Liverpool, London (Imperial College), Manchester, Oxford and Sheffield.

"We found in fact", Ken Woodward commented, "that about 12 universities provided some 80 per cent of our graduate intake. On the other hand, we were not looking for bench boffins. We wanted a good degree plus the ability to communicate where research scientists were concerned, and the same in the case of engineers. For non-technical posts, such as marketing, we were looking for general intelligence plus personality."

The Courtauld approach to the Milk Round differs only in detail from that of other leading companies; and despite or perhaps because of the recession, more and more firms are getting involved in the Round.

"There is a broad split between technical and non-technical recruitment", Ken Woodward noted, "or, if you like, between specialist and non-specialist. Science, engineering and law students, for example, command the same interest as ever,

100

but now the retail sector, especially the big supermarkets, and accountancy firms are recruiting increasingly from the universities. The arts man, given numeracy, is being recruited for training in cost and works accountancy, while the traditional arts man continues to go into personnel work, administration, marketing and now, retail."

On the question of political attitudes and the much publicised hostility to capitalism among university students, Woodward took the view that there seemed to be less of a Left-wing attitude abroad on the campuses today, but that of course public sector jobs were becoming fewer and fewer. "In any case," he observed, "if students apply to a company's blandishments in the first place, that in itself is a kind of 'filter'. At the same time there are still a great number of students who have no idea what industry's all about."

Not a cheap operation
The cost of recruiting from universities may strike some people as surprisingly high, though a very high proportion of it is represented by fixed costs such as literature, visits to universities and a somewhat liberal use of personnel staff and resources. This being the case, it can cost almost as much to interview 50 as 100 students, and in Woodward's experience, "it is not unusual for the cost of recruiting one graduate to be in the region of £2,000." This is only the merest fraction of what a headhunter may charge for finding an outstanding executive, nevertheless it may raise a few eyebrows.

The Milk Round, on the other hand, is an effective recruiting tool for the market concerned, and Woodward agrees with Dibden that it is difficult to think of an alternative approach. "The graduate has the benefit of the service being brought to him", he commented, "and the results have usually been confirmed by experience. Indeed, a high percentage of senior managers have come into industry via the Milk Round route, and the company with a coherent management development policy benefits most of all."

Benefiting least of all from the Milk Round, as already

noted, is the small firm, except of course the small, high professional firm — engineers, architects, accountants and the like — seeking specialist staff. Part of the problem is that companies of modest size are often unable to provide the sophisticated selection and training facilities which help to recruit the right person in the first place and make the best use of him (or her) after he has joined the payroll. Another reason is that owners of small businesses just do not think in terms of graduates where certain jobs are concerned or, conversely, may expect Superman because the recruit in question happens to have a degree.

"The employer's attitude can in fact be the greatest problem of all", Kenneth Dibden claims. "Small firms new to the Milk Round often expect more of a graduate than he can offer. They assume that the award of a degree means that he is professionally trained and able to 'manage', so they may be disappointed because they misunderstand what they are buying, and expect immediate results."

Degree dazzle

Small employers, however, are not the only people to suffer from degree dazzle. Even Dibden claims that "the award of a degree does mean that the recipient is capable of high achievement, of meeting standards set by others and of learning quickly. The graduate is likely to have a developed personality, judgement, determination and analytical powers. Perhaps most important, he knows how to tackle a problem."

In my own opinion, recruiters and employers do well to circle warily round a university degree lest they mistake it for a copper-bottomed guarantee of future achievement. The American President, Calvin Coolidge, did not cut a scintillating figure at the White House, but he deserves to be remembered for pointing out that the world is full of "educated derelicts" and that nothing is more common than unsuccessful men with talent. Or, in the words of Professor Alex MacFie, of Glasgow University, to members of his class who had just graduated: "Let me tell you this before you go into the world to seek your fortunes. Brains are ten a penny: what counts above all is character."

This is not meant as an attack on academic achievement but as a plea to see it in perspective. It can be regarded as proof of above average intelligence and even of the ability to complete a task once begun. But I would not say that it is an earnest of high future achievement; given an above average I.Q. and an indulgent examiner, even the most idle student can end up with a scroll containing Gothic lettering.

Having made that point, it is nevertheless difficult to say where else firms large and small should look for their executive talent of the future. Selection at all levels, be it on the Milk Round or at international headhunter level, is an elitist activity which helps to consolidate the elitist truth that people are not born equal, however desirable it may be that they should enjoy something approaching equal opportunity. Employers may occasionally discover some youth straight from school who has it in him to become a highly successful chief executive, but such examples are now as rare as pork chops in Mecca or Jerusalem. The so-called "enlightened" approach to education which we are witnessing in the United Kingdom today, with its rejection of literacy and numeracy as class concepts (in both senses), is steadily eroding both the apprenticeship and grammar school routes by which so many able young people won a start in commerce and industry. The way to the top must thus lead mainly through the universities and polytechnics, but that does not mean that even the most brilliant double firsts have it within them to be Arnold Weinstock or Freddie Laker.

Yet the stock of basic raw material out of which executive talent is fashioned must constantly be added to. Headhunters themselves claim that their activities disturb the fatal long-term effects of executive homeostasis and get talent circulating, thereby creating more room at the top. This, however, is not a human parallel to the Quantity Theory of Money, whereby the faster money is made to circulate, the less of it is needed to serve the national economy. There is an absolute shortage of executive talent

103

in the world of today — probably there always was — and it has to be searched not only in a competitor's boardroom but in what are referred to sometimes as "the groves of Academe". That is the significance of the Milk Round, and the main problem is to help small firms to get a fair share of the action.

9
Ways of Picking Winners

> Conceal yoursel as weel's ye can
> Frae critical dissection,
> But keek thro' every other man
> Wi' sharpened sly inspection.

Haloes and bumps

These lines from Robert Burns' *Epistle to a Young Friend* might well have been written with headhunters especially in mind, if the breed had existed in the late 18th century. Whether or not the recruitment industry of today is any more percipient than their counterparts of the early days of the Industrial Revolution is a moot point: there can be no doubt, however, that the search and selection men of today have at their command all manner of aids which, with one or two exceptions, simply were not available in those earlier times — or, if available, were not geared to the needs of commerce and industry.

It is tempting to say that the aids to selection available today range from the ridiculous to the sublime, but perhaps it would be more accurate to say "from the exotic to the pragmatic". Moving from left to right along the spectrum, as it were, we have techniques such as Kirlian photography (which purports to be a means of taking snap shots of people's auras), astrology, chirology (which is palmistry in a white coat), graphology, action profiling (or the study of human movements), personality and intelligence testing and, finally, the common-or-garden interview. In the nature of things, some of these are used very, very sparingly, but it may strike some people as curious that they are used at all. It would be wrong, however, to think of recruiters as people of transcendental scepticism, like most others, they have their weaknesses and enthusiasms. True, I have yet to hear of a headhunter who employs Kirlian photography as a means of separating sheep from goats, nor any associated techniques such as phrenology or physiognomy, but for those who may be interested Kirlian was a Soviet scientist who invented a camera which, it was claimed, was capable of taking pictures of the halo or "luminous plasma" which allegedly surrounds human beings. I saw slides of such "pictures" a few years ago at a management conference; they were, to say the least, highly unusual, and I left with the uncomfortable feeling that I would not have liked my own halo to be visible to a living soul.

Stars and palms
Kirlian photography apart, however, some of the other techniques mentioned are much more commonly used than one would suppose. Astrology, for instance, is widely employed as an aid to selection in the Far East and to some extent in France as well. For instance, Sheila MacLeod, a further education teacher, developed a series of courses in the subject on behalf of the Inner London Education Authority (ILEA); these courses were aimed in particular at users of data processing systems. Personal horoscopes, she maintains, are based on "the correlations between the individual and extra-terrestrial phenomena", and can provide the experienced astrologer with information about "the physical and psychological identity of the individual". Moreover, she claims that the process can validate "statements made by the interviewee regarding early background, schooling, work record and present circumstances."

More specifically, Sheila MacLeod maintains that, by examining any function within an organisation and identifying the type of people who are successful in that function, the astrologer can determine from a sample of birth charts "the astrological factors that correlate with success at any given time". Success, she stresses, depends as much on getting on with the group as being able to cope with the technical demands of the job, and astrology "helps to define the essence of these inter-relationships".

To the person who knows what he likes and likes what he knows, poking fun at astrology is often as easy as, to use the old Glaswegian simile, "taking toffee off a wean". We are confidently informed by astronomers, however, that the atoms making up the universe are in gravitational balance, so it may be wise not to dismiss out of hand the notion that our individual lives can be affected by gravitational forces.

Chirology, likewise, is one of those topics on which it may be prudent to keep an open mind, but first we must rid our minds of the image of the fortune teller's booth at the fairground. Dr Rowan Bayne, a psychologist on the Civil Service Selection Board, describes the technique as "a very speculative area of study, which involves looking at the way hands are held, also at the backs of hands, at their size, shape and degree of pinkness as well as at the lines on their palms."

"There are two complementary approaches", he explains, "namely, the technical and the emotional intuitive. My own interest is in the technical and is based on the assumption that physique and personality is genetically expressed. For example, it is thought that thin angular people love solitude and that a long little finger indicates managerial ability."

At any rate, chirologists believe that an intimate link exists between the brain and the hands because of the large number of nerve endings in the latter. In theory, then, the lines of the hands should vanish with death, and there is in fact some evidence that these lines do begin to break down when cerebral impulses cease.

As to the connection between chirology and selection, the "professional" view is that one can measure personality, abilities and the general state of an individual's health from

107

characteristics of the hands. In Dr Bayne's view, however, it would take two to three hours to assess a candidate for a senior management post by this method and in any case all the existing evidence can do at this stage "is to make palmistry slightly more feasible". More tests and pilot studies are urgently needed, if this area of enquiry is to be seriously pursued.

'Brain writing'

Graphology, to mix a metaphor, is a different kettle of fish, and is much more widely used in the selection field than may be supposed; in particular, it is very popular in Germany, Switzerland, France and Scandinavia. Indeed, in some parts of Europe, graphology is now being taught as a post-graduate subject, not in connection with science but as a tool for psychological testing and assessment.

"Handwriting", maintains Sam Smith, principal psychologist of Austin Knight Appointments Ltd, a leading London firm in the recruitment advertising field, "is both a conscious and unconscious activity. It is controlled by the personality and should really be called 'brain writing'. For instance, when an applicant fills in a form or writes a letter, he gives consciously the information he wants to give, but in addition he unconsciously exposes his personality."

Sam Smith claims that this is "betrayed" by such details as the size of the letters, the degree of pressure in the strokes, in how the "i" dots and the "t" strokes are placed, in the use of space and margins and the like.

"Furthermore", he stresses, "handwriting can never be static. It changes, and should change, according to the age and emotional state of the person at the time of writing. Analysis is thus extremely complex and, although each symbol can be interpreted on its own, it is meaningless if it cannot be interpreted in a wholistic, statistically validated pattern."

As proof of how an individual's personality and emotional condition can affect handwriting, Sam Smith quotes, among other examples, the deteriorating signature of President Nixon as the Watergate crisis became more and more acute. Shortly before his resignation, the President's signature had become practically "inarticulate", a vague, incoherent scribble.

In the opinion of Smith and other graphologists, handwriting highlights all manner of human qualities from extreme boldness — often seen in the hand of the potential high flyer — to the extreme caution of the timid and unimaginative, and from the euphoria of the psychotic to the inner conflict of the neurotic. It can also identify a whole range of behaviour patterns, including honesty and dishonesty and even the profession of the individual. "In fact", Sam Smith stresses, "the signatures of the confidence trickster and the professional man are not always wholly dissimilar."

Which may not seem in the least surprising to some people.

Among the case histories cited by Smith to underline the value of graphology is one concerning 30 vacancies for qualified engineers for which there had been 400 eligible applicants. In the ordinary way, this would have been a six months' interviewing task. However, by defining the personality factors vital to each job, and by studying the handwriting of each applicant in relation to these factors, it was possible to eliminate 200 of the applicants.

"The exercise proved to be successful", Smith added, "both in the quality of the final appointees and in terms of financial savings."

Another case history concerned an African industrial training organisation which found that more than half of the candidates whom it had sent to British technical colleges for engineering training had either failed to pass their examinations or could not settle after having returned home. By analysing three handwriting samples from all former trainees (on initial application, after the first year and upon return) the writing of fresh applicants could be compared with the distinctive features of that of the successes and failures. On this basis, only the likely successes were sent for training, and as a result the "fall out rate" was cut by half.

Sam Smith speaks for the practitioners as a whole when he says that "in the hands of responsible professionals, graphology will be wrested from the grip of the charlatans and the pseudo-sciences to become a valuable tool for psychological assessment." Certainly it is one of the most credible of what may be termed "the fringe aids to selection" and its use among British selection consultants seems to be growing slowly but steadily. Even so, the technique would appear to be faced with a long and difficult road as far as British industry is concerned. According to the findings of the BIM/IPM survey, only about 1% of respondent firms admitted to using graphology as a selection aid. Small wonder Sam Smith himself thinks that it could be fifty years before it becomes an established part of psychological testing in this country!

Moving experience

From handwriting to general physical movement moves the spotlight towards the technique known as Management Action Profiling (MAP), a service which has been available in the United Kingdom since the early 1950s through the firm of Warren Lamb Associates. For all that its director, Warren Lamb, claims that thousands of managers have been action-profiled, the technique, which analyzes the candidate's movements during interview, is little known even in managerial circles.

"Currently", Warren Lamb points out, "there are only seven fully-trained action profilers in Europe and the U.S.A. but more are being trained and they include senior personnel managers and management development advisers."

MAP, as stated, consists in assessing personality through an analysis of the individual's movements. According to Warren Lamb, each individual has a pattern of movement which is constant and enduring, so that it can be said to be characteristic of the person concerned. "It is revealing", he maintains, "because it does not depend on conditioning, as with some other aspects of behaviour." The movements themselves may appear to be of little significance to the untrained observer: for example, shifting about in the chair, stroking one's chin, drumming fingers on the desk, tapping the feet, craning forward, smoothing one's hair are not likely to attract much attention unless done non-stop. Lamb, however, claims that body movements can reveal aspects of people which could not be gained from any other source. Moreover, it is his contention — upon which hinges a successful business — that such movements can be interpreted in a form relevant to management selection.

Or if one prefers the term, action profiling is the study of non-verbal behaviour. What happens is that the "profiler" sits unobtrusively in the office where the interview is taking place, and notes down the candidate's movement in a kind of shorthand code, afterwards supplying the client with a report on the candidate's suitability or lack of it for the job in question based on his interpretation of his notes.

Warren Lamb developed his techniques after training with the leading movement theorist of his day, Rudolf Laban, then opened his own consultancy in London in 1952, since when, he says, he has been constantly refining the technique. Among his current clients are the General Electric Company, National Coal Board, Rank Corporation, Colgate Palmolive and the Dunlop Group, and he points out that some executives recruited through his methods more than 20 years ago are still in the same posts.

An MAP interview may last between two and three hours, during which a candidate may make anything between 50 and 500 movements of interest to the action profiler — the more the better, says Lamb. Such movements are assessed in 12 different categories, leading to an action profile which, it is claimed, cannot be faked. Even if a candidate is interviewed on different days and in different moods, the resulting profile will be consistent because it identifies enduring and not temporary characteristics. "For instance", Lamb explains, "nervousness does not affect the profile."

MAP, according to Warren Lamb Associates, is not only an effective aid to selection but can be and is also used for what he calls "top team planning". As the phrase implies, the technique is used in this case to action profile members of an existing management team to provide an assessment and advice about the balance of the team in relation to the type of decisions which have to be taken in the business concerned. Training in the technique is also offered. This ranges from two-day briefing seminars for senior executives to a one-year programme in MAP including supervised training both on and off the job and tailored to the specific job environment of the student. Successful completion of the course, says Lamb, qualifies the trainee to become a fully-fledged MAP practitioner.

There was a time, Lamb admits, when action profiling was regarded as "way out" but in recent years he claims that it has been gaining steadily in "respectability".

Such may well be the case, and also in that of the other selection nostrums discussed in this chapter so far. Yet if the extent of their use in headhunting circles can be regarded as a measure of their intrinsic worth, then all the techniques in the left band of the spectrum have to be rejected as suspect or of academic interest only. This, however, is not an entirely valid deduction, and it is worth bearing in mind that there was a time not so long ago when headhunting itself was regarded as highly suspect. Personally, I am convinced that both graphology and MAP have something of real value for the recruiter, though my native scepticism takes over when it comes to "keeking" at auras, maps of the hands and the juxtapositions of heavenly bodies. Yet even at this level it is as well to remember that Napoleon's main yardstick when it came to appointing senior officers was the question — "Is this man lucky?" And it seemed to work for a time at least. Again, it is no more ridiculous to be hooked on astrology than to select on the basis of "I can tell if he's any good the moment he walks through the door" — which is an attitude still all too prevalent among employers.

'Shrinking' territory

In moving into the band occupied by personality, intelligence and aptitude testing, we forsake the exotic for more familiar territory. It has been estimated that some five to seven per cent of British firms use testing of this kind, though, according to the BIM/IPM survey, 21% of respondents thought intelligence and personality tests could be "useful" while 26% held the same opinion of aptitude tests. Testing of this kind is also fairly widely used among selection consultants and, less frequently, by search consultants.

"We've our own psychologists on the payroll", commented Garry Long of Management Selection Ltd, "and in the U.S.A. we test all shortlisted candidates. Here in the United Kingdom it all depends on the client, while in Germany they seem to be sold on graphology."

Some of the leading headhunting firms throughout the world also make regular use of personality and intelligence testing. According to Douglas MacKenzie Davey, one of Britain's top industrial psychologists, "One of our roles is to inspect the products of headhunters, who will perhaps send three candidates on a shortlist to us. They spend a day with us, during which we submit them to personality and intelligence testing, but we don't lean too heavily on tests. Interviewing is just as important, and although of course we don't probe as deeply as a psychoanalyst, we are very interested in the candidate's childhood and personal history. Afterwards I prepare a report for the client (see appendix to this chapter) covering three main areas: the candidate's likely behaviour under pressure; the conclusions from our testing; and the way he is likely to relate with others. I like to think that the client is by then able to come to a decision, but I go on to relate the candidate to the job."

MacKenzie Davey went on to say that his consultancy dealt with a very wide range of clients, most of them in respect of top jobs such as managing director or other board level appointments. "Some clients, I.T.T. for example, also use us for internal promotion", he added. "Indeed, I would say that about one-third of those we see are company-sponsored, and sometimes client firms do this to assess us! Or, again, we may test people in whom the client is going to invest a lot of money, say, in training."

Contrasting his approach with that of the search and selection industry, MacKenzie Davey said that headhunters were more interested in track records — i.e. in the past — whereas he was more interested in how candidates were likely to perform in the future. "In general", he went on, "I would say that the big companies are cutting back in their use of people like ourselves because of the recession but we are now acting for a lot of newer and smaller clients. The recession, however, has exposed a lot of the deadwood, and I would agree that there does seem to be a real shortage of executive talent. In my experience, the two main weaknesses are lack of intellectual calibre and lack of toughness, so that lack of stability becomes a problem."

The type of service provided by consultancies such as MacKenzie Davey's is not cheap, but many headhunters consider the £350-£400 a day charged by such experts to be money well spent, to be an ideal method of preparing the final shortlist before presentation to the client. Of headhunters themselves, he is on record as saying: "They are the grey men; they have to be. After all, they're trying to be spies, so it's no use being memorable. They used to be a bit funny about visiting cards, even. Didn't carry them in case they got left in the wrong offices. One characteristic . . . they're great gossips, and they go about their business with the same enthusiasm as the matchmaker."

In the course of talking to many headhunters, I have come across little or no evidence which confirms or refutes this assessment. True, most headhunters are ready talkers (but then so are journalists and marketing men) though none of them ever said anything indiscreet to me without verifying first that it was off the record. Again, whilst I met none who dresses like a punk rocker or a clown on stilts, few of them suggest the subfusc, dry as dust civil servant either as regards attire or personality, nor did I glean the impression that, figuratively, they are in the habit of looking over their shoulders before vouchsafing an opinion. As far as I have been able to judge, they are like any other group of managers, though perhaps a little too "paranoid" about what the competition is up to.

This, however, is to digress. Some very interesting and important views on psychological testing as it applies to recruitment are given by John Wareham, president of John Wareham Associates, a leading international headhunting consultancy with headquarters in New York, in his book *Secrets of a Corporate Headhunter*, the burden of his message being that; "On its own, *any* form of psychological testing however sophisticated, and whatever the qualifications of the interpreter, is like trying to guess what a person looks like by studying his shadow: results vary according to the position of the diagnostician, the quarry and the sun."

Wareham, who writes from long experience and outstanding achievement, dismisses utterly "objective" personality testing in which a computer is pressed into service to analyze little ticks in boxes, "thus relieving management of the need to make a decision." He is a little more lenient, however, towards projective personality tests whereby the subject is invited to describe what he sees in an inkblot, picture or whatever, or to complete a sentence. He sees these tests as an extension of the interview and as a means of eliciting the candidate's values, but at the same time "the decision-making process is pushed to where it belongs — out of the computer and on to the desk of the senior executive."

As to intelligence tests, Wareham is against these for three reasons. "First", he points out, "there is no necessary correlation between high intelligence and good judgement, and some intellectually gifted people lack any capacity whatsoever to make executive decisions."

"Second, you can painlessly establish how smart an executive is simply by studying his record. That he completed a bona fide college degree is an infinitely better guide to his intelligence — and his motivation — than practically any test result . . ."

"Third, the whole concept of intelligence testing is inflammatory and now has so many EEOC (Equal Employment Opportunity Commission, which requires that women be given every chance in management echelons) implications that you might as well steer clear of the whole subject."

Of course, although John Wareham is one of the world's leading headhunters, that does not necessarily qualify him to be the final authority on psychological testing, nor even does the deftness of his prose or the vividness of his imagery. On the other hand, the actual content of what he says is so eminently sensible that it is hard to dispute. His insights are those of an intelligent man who has operated successfully in the highly competitive American market, and who no doubt has learned the hard way of the gap which often yawns between brain power and actual performance. Clearly, too, if personality and intelligence testing were all that was needed to choose executives for key posts, personnel departments would have learned long since to administer such tests and there would be no need for a recruitment industry as we know it today.

At the same time, tests and interviews by experienced industrial psychologists are obviously valuable as an element in the search or selection process. As the appendix to this chapter shows, (published here with the kind permission of Douglas MacKenzie Davey) testing of this kind enables the recruiter to make finer, more precise appraisals of short-listed candidates, and where the future profits of a company may rest upon a successful appointment, precision of this kind could be crucial. Moreover, psychological testing has obvious benefits to offer personnel departments in the area of internal promotion and management development. Yet it must always be seen for what it is — as a walking stick rather than a crutch.

Again, despite all the techniques which are available to the recruiter, one of the most persistent myths in the whole appraisal process is that one can tell a good or bad candidate just by looking at him. Even MacKenzie Davey is on record as saying, "The routine tests give me a sound base to work on, but I can tell just from the look of the man that there's something wrong with his liver — or the equivalent."

There is more to this faith in first impressions than meets

the eye, so to speak. As Schopenhauer pointed out in one of his *Psychological Observations*, when we see someone for the first time, we see that person without any "interference" from past association with him or her; neither the mind, the emotions nor the physical senses has been prejudiced against or in favour of the subject, and as a result we see the person as he or she really is. Even so, it is worth checking out what we see.

Eyeball to eyeball

It is not surprising that the interview, backed up by a study and assessment of the candidate's track record, should be favoured in the United Kingdom (and indeed elsewhere) as by far the most popular method of selecting executives. It is estimated, in fact, that more than 90% of British companies rely on this approach, although the very largest undertakings, especially the multi-nationals, often combine the interview with other selection techniques. According to the BIM/IPM survey, for example, panel selection boards are used by 15% to 20% of companies but the ratio increases to one in three in companies with more than 5,000 employees. As for group selection methods, such as are applied in the case of the Administrative Class of the Civil Service, these are thought to be used by up to 5% of companies but to be most suited to graduate recruitment, and of course I have already noted in this chapter that many large firms make use of industrial psychologists for "objective" appraisal tests. Group selection techniques are rarely if ever used at all, however, in the selection of middle and senior executives.

All this is very much in keeping with the British empiric tradition, which eschews theory and intellectual speculation in favour of commonsense and experience fortified perhaps by an underlying emotional need to play one's hunches and to get a good look at the goods on display. John Wareham's point about the need to look at more than the candidate's shadow is well taken. The need to see and talk with a candidate is so obvious as to need no elaborating here, save to say that only in this way can we form any intuitions about another person — and although it may be impossible to articulate our intuitions, this does not make them any the less valid. "I do not like thee, Dr Fell", etc.

Certainly, in the case of search and selection consultants, track record plus personal interview(s) take priority over all other methods. "The appraisal of candidates varies from company to company", states Bert Young, chairman of Alexander Hughes & Associates (UK) Ltd, "and from headhunter to headhunter, but the common factor is the one that has so far proved to be alone in having any predictive value and that is past performance. Unhappily even that is only a necessary and not a sufficient condition for suitability. So a wide range of supplementary hoops have been put up for the candidate to jump through, and these have been known to include psychological tests, depth interviews, graphology, medical examinations and personality tests."

In Young's opinion, all this underlines the value of using an outsider to screen out the best men, since it is a time-consuming task and "senior management time should be devoted to running the company". He also insists that the ability to run a business does not necessarily include the ability to choose men. Perhaps not, but it usually does; a much more common condition is where the ability to run a business does not include the gift of being liked personally.

Strong support for the interview method comes from Nigel Rugman, director of Management Appointments Ltd, who claims that, whilst an interview offers little time in which to judge technical competence, ability, personality and motivation, it is nevertheless "the best means of making value judgements." He also maintains that "quasi-scientific, psychological and other methods of testing, although sometimes useful as additional sources of reference, are no substitute for exercising your own judgement." He also dismisses panel interviewing as a thoroughly sterile occupation, "while stress techniques are of value only to interrogators".

Having winnowed out the chaff, Rugman looks at the grain of interviewing, stressing that the best examples consist of a natural conversation between headhunter and candidate.

"In such an unpressurised setting", he claims, "the candidate is most likely to show his true qualities." He goes on to stress that "half the purpose of an interview is to persuade the candidate that your company and job are appropriate to his needs", and suggests that dinner provides an ideal informal environment for the candidate who is finally selected either to confirm his suitability for the appointment or to reveal previously hidden flaws. One would have thought this perhaps a little late for any such revelations.

Anyhow, Nigel Rugman was certainly speaking for the headhunting tribe as a whole when he said that "recruitment consultancy is not about novel techniques but about the competence with which the standard methodology is employed." Garry Long of M.S.L. noted "a lot of resistance in the United Kingdom to unusual selection techniques" while R.A.B. Gowlland of Egon Zehnder International said that his own company made little or no use of "original" or "unconventional" techniques, and went on to liken the whole process to Carlyle's famous dictum about "the infinite capacity for taking pains".

Much the same approach was quoted by Anthony Langdon, chairman of Eurosurvey Ltd, who stressed that "our whole operation is based upon massive research and for that reason we will contact anything between 100 and 300 candidates initially by 'phone on an individual assignment, and we think nothing, for example, of working a 12-hour day and taking the evening shuttle from Heathrow to Scotland to have dinner with a candidate. Setting up the research is by far the most difficult part of the job, after which the rest falls into place. Another vital area is the job description, which in our documentation runs to three pages: page one describes the company, page two deals with the job, and page three describes the man the client would like."

With external recruitment, then, it is clear that the interview is very often the culminating phase of a process which begins with the job description and continues through the search or advertising phase, and as such cannot be considered in isolation. In 1980, incidentally, Eurosurvey Ltd carried out a survey covering the United Kingdom, Holland, Belgium, France and the German Federal Republic into *Recruiting Top Management and Directors for the Smaller to Medium-Sized Company,* in the course of which questionnaires were sent to 3,500 companies from whom a 16% response was obtained. The findings indicated that executive search was the most frequently used method of external recruitment in the U.K., a claim which certainly conflicts with the findings of the BIM/IPM survey, which said that only 4% of British companies used headhunters and only 14% used selection consultants. Readers may nevertheless wish to study the Eurosurvey Ltd figures, which are as follows:-

Methods of External Recruitment

Method	France	Belgium	Holland	UK	W Germany
Executive search	29	16	26	34	8
Personal contact	27	41	33	31	39
Advertisements in coy. name	15	22	29	19	35
Agency advertisements	22	20	12	14	18
Other	7	1	—	2	—

It will be noted that, according to the above findings, 65% of all external recruitment in the U.K. is based on direct approach methods.

Moreover, Eurosurvey Ltd goes on to state that in all countries the highest importance in the whole selection process, so the response says, is given to the personality of the candidate — which, by implication, argues that the interview is the key feature in the process. "Innate potential, i.e. general calibre and work experience, are seen to be the next most important selection criteria", the report continues, "but far less importance is given to educational attainment and to the ability to make an effective contribution very quickly. No importance was given to age and language abilities."

Survey findings or no, these conclusions — to put it mildly — will not command universal assent among head-hunters. Yet if what I have been told by leading search consultants about the importance of the individual's personal chemistry and of "fitting in" is true, then surely personality must rank at least equally with "track record" and "ability to make a quick contribution". On the other hand, it seems impossible to me that potential employers should ascribe no importance to age.

As to the alleged indifference among employers to linguistic ability, Eurosurvey Ltd makes the following, very interesting point:

". . . although this answer is the same throughout Europe, the reasons for the answer are different. On the continent, most senior managers take language skills for granted and hence not worth a comment, whereas in the U.K. the need for them tends to be discounted." (The company adds that this finding had been established in an earlier survey.)

It is interesting to compare the Eurosurvey findings on qualities sought with those of the BIM/IPM report on *Selecting Managers*. "The three most highly valued qualities", said the latter, "are: motivation, contribution to the job and ability to get on with colleagues." The survey also revealed that personal factors were seen as subordinate to ability factors in the case of specialist jobs but as paramount in the case of middle and senior management, where qualities such as "leadership" and ability to work as a member of a team were seen as vital.

But to return to the relative importance of the interview. In British management circles, apart from the commonsense view that the interview remains the best way of getting to know the candidate, there seems also to be a distinct bias (conscious or otherwise) against the use of tests, especially where middle and senior executive appointments are

121

concerned. Tests may be appropriate in the case of graduates or for specialist jobs such as in computing or marketing, but, to quote the BIM/IPM survey, "there is a feeling that the use of other selection methods, such as tests, is somehow un-British." In plain language, this probably means "We think it un-British to check out the claims you made on your application form and at the interview, so we must use our own judgement instead." It is only fair to point out, however, that the bias against testing does not exist so strongly in other parts of the Western world, neither among clients nor candidates.

Yet the curious fact is that the executives who have the greatest say in deciding whom shall be appointed have usually had little or no training in the art of interviewing. At the same time, more than 90% of British companies (and headhunters too for that matter) rely almost entirely on the interview when recruiting, though the larger companies and the multi-nationals do employ a greater variety of selection methods. "Considering that few companies have much experience of any other method", commented the BIM/IPM survey, "it is hardly remarkable that interviewing is generally considered to be the most useful selection method. As many as 95% of the companies ranked interviewing as useful and panel interviews by selection boards were ranked second in order of usefulness (45% of companies so rated these). Other methods (leaving aside medicals) are not held to be particularly useful although psychologists will no doubt be relieved to see that tests fare considerably better than graphology."

As to medical examinations, an extraordinary feature is that, according to the same survey, only between 25% and 28% of the companies responding insisted on medicals. The headhunter himself of course cannot insist on these but the general view among them is that the client ought to do so. More than one admitted to me of case histories where the first choice of both headhunter and client had been an executive with less than a year to live!

But possibly the most remarkable aspect of the blind

faith which top managers in the United Kingdom seem to place in the interview is that it seems to work in most cases. Unless he is called in as some kind of company doctor or surgeon, what outsider has the right to say who or what is best for the business in question? Perhaps "fitting in" *is* to be preferred to an instant contribution, especially in these days of "democratic" management when it can cost a fortune to get rid of someone. Or maybe most managements have the nous to realise that it is impossible in any case to make a contribution without first being acceptable as a member of the management team. And the interview is the only way of "sussing out" whether a candidate has the right chemistry. Even so, it is hoped that the appendix which follows will say something in support of psychological assessment as well.

It was Sam Goldwyn who is supposed to have said that "a guy who visits a psychiatrist ought to have his head examined", and maybe the same applies with muted relevance to those who seek the counsel of psychologists. It seems to me, however, that the Specimen Report printed here is the type of document which reveals human strengths and weaknesses that might well escape even the shrewdest and most highly trained interviewer at a run-of-the-mill meeting. As already noted, leading industrial psychologists charge between £350 and £400 per day for their services, but many firms already consider this to be money well spent when it comes to recruiting for posts which can affect the profitability – or, indeed, the survival – of the enterprise.

SPECIMEN REPORT

Mr. A.B. Smith

Confidential Assessment

by

D. Mackenzie Davey

1 March 1978

This is a CONFIDENTIAL management report.

It should be shown only to those responsible for making decisions about the individual concerned. Under no circumstances should it be shown to him or its contents discussed with him.

If you have any questions, please do not hesitate to get in touch with the assessor.

PERSONAL MAKE UP

Note: This report is concerned primarily with judgements
about how the candidate will behave at work. It
does not concern itself with the reasons why he
will behave in any particular way; nor does it
comment on technical or professional competence.

INTELLECTUAL EFFECTIVENESS

Note: Comparisons are made below with the "management
population". This is a highly selected group of
senior managers who represent, in terms of their
intellectual capacity, approximately the top
seven per cent of the general population.

Synopsis

Mr. Smith's basic intelligence places him a little below
the average for managers.

(i)   Numerical
He worked quickly but inaccurately on a numerically
based reasoning test and his score was below average
— at a level which would be bettered by two out
of three managers.

(ii)   Verbal
His score on a test of verbal comprehension was
substantially above average. He has a large
vocabulary which he deploys effectively in both
speech and writing. His fluency is impressive and
could lead to an over-estimation of his intellectual
power.

(iii)   Logical
On tests of various aspects of "critical" thinking
his performance was undistinguished and placed
him well below the management average. He is a
man who tends to allow his feelings to influence his
judgement: he would have more difficulty than most
managers in analysing them objectively and dis-
passionately. He will act on intuition and frequently
allow his personal views to influence his judgement.

(iv)   Imaginative
He responded fluently to tests of "productive"
thinking and produced an above average number of
ideas. The evidence suggests that, faced with novel or
unexpected problems, he will not be at a loss and
he could produce some imaginative ideas.

APPENDIX – SPECIMEN REPORT

WORK APPROACH

(i) General Approach
     He is an energetic man who tackles his work with
     vigour and drive.

(ii) Mastery of Detail
      He does not see it as important to have a thorough
      knowledge of the minor matters for which he is
      responsible. Indeed, in order to achieve what he
      saw as his primary objectives, he would tend to
      dismiss many matters as trivial or as irrelevant
      detail.

(iii) Productivity
       He is hard-working. He is able to sustain his efforts
       and will generally put through a good deal of work
       in a comparatively short time: his output will be
       high.

(iv) Quality of Work
      He can work faster than most managers, and he will
      sometimes sacrifice accuracy for speed; thus,
      although his output will be substantial it will not
      always be of the highest quality.

(v) Decision Making
     He is optimistic and rather impetuous. He will make
     swift positive decisions. Those concerned with
     concrete, tangible problems will usually be sensible
     but his judgement on matters of policy or broad
     strategy must be suspect.

(vi) Tolerance for Pressure
      Mr. Smith does not appear to be well equipped to
      work under extended pressure. He is not emotionally
      robust and his capacity to tolerate more than
      moderate stress is questionable. He will act swiftly,
      but not always intelligently, in a crisis.

(vii) Flexibility
       There is a restlessness in his make up which gives
       him the flexibility to adapt to new situations and
       to accept changes of priority without complaining.
       But the same restlessness makes him bored with
       routine work and intolerant of tasks calling for
       steady application. This factor has probably
       contributed to his relatively frequent job changes
       over the last twelve years.

(viii) Ambition
He is ambitious and prepared to make sacrifices
in order to progress. He hopes to be chief executive
of a medium-sized organisation or to have a senior
executive role in a large one — both are a little
unrealistic. He can, in the right environment, be
a competent middle manager, but he is unlikely to
be successful in a top position.

RELATIONSHIPS WITH OTHERS

(i) General Impact
Mr. Smith uses his verbal skills to present himself
positively but he tends to be a little over-zealous
in displaying his charm and, especially over longer
periods, is likely to be seen as rather superficial
in his personal relationships. Thus, while first
impressions can be excellent they may not be
sustained.

(ii) Relationships with Superiors
His seniors will find him a mixture of amenability
and stubbornness. He will communicate his views
lucidly and often contribute constructively, but
there will be times when he will be unable to conceal
his anxiety and will behave in an ill-judged manner.
He could, for example, appear frivolous at
inappropriate times — he uses laughter to escape
from difficult situations — and at other times he will
be obstinate and aggressive.

(iii) Relationships with Peers
He would not be a particularly good man in a team;
he is inclined to be over-critical of the views of
his associates and over-sure of the rightness of
his own judgement. Moreover, he would become
impatient if subjected to the delays imposed by
committee work. He is action-centred and he
becomes frustrated and irritable if unable to
implement his ideas.

He lacks the stability and personal security to
develop mature relationships. Most especially his
high degrees of sensitivity will lead him to see
slights where none are intended and to treat the
most neutral of situations with suspicion.

(iv) Relationships with Subordinates
He would make earnest efforts to manage others
with authority but may not always be able to sustain
his status. He has underlying doubts about his own
capacities and these will sometimes become evident
in his direct dealings with subordinates. On the

other hand, he would often be seen as a positive and cheerful manager, and, when not obsessed with his own feelings and sensitivities, would show an awareness of the problems of others. Moreover, his instructions will be lucid and unambiguous.

PRIMARY ASSETS

Industrious and energetic
Flexible; can adapt to change
Decisive
Above average ability to communicate clearly
Imaginative
Makes a good first impression

PRIMARY LIMITATIONS

Basic intellectual power a little below average
Judgement of emotionally toned situations suspect
   – analytical skills below average
Unstable and insecure – doubtful capacity to
   tolerate extended stress
Hypersensitive – quick to take offence
Unable to sustain seemingly friendly, cheerful
   manner
Not at his best in a team

GUIDELINES FOR DEVELOPMENT

Mr. Smith needs the support of a well structured environment and clearly defined duties to give him stability. His methods of working and limits of authority should be agreed in advance. He should be encouraged to develop his analytical skills: he will never be a gifted logician but he could become rather less subjective in his judgements than he is at present.

SUMMARY

Mr. Smith has many admirable characteristics – in particular his energy and drive, his communication skills, and his decisiveness. Against these must be weighed his distinctly limited emotional stability and his modest intellectual resources.

He presents himself skilfully but he is unable to sustain the positive impression that he makes. In his efforts to do so his manner comes to appear rather forced and false. Moreover, he is an extremely sensitive man who would detect in the most innocent of actions or statements by others a criticism or even an insult. In consequence, his relationships with his associates are likely to deteriorate considerably.

Handling familiar tasks he could be relied upon to act sensibly and incisively. This often impressive performance could lead to a general over-estimation of his abilities and the temptation to give him more demanding duties which would, in many cases, be beyond him. He is very close to his limits and while he could do a competent job at one stage higher than his present one he is unlikely to be effective in top positions.

10
Management's Forgotten Men

Guilty without trial

Redundant executives do not loom large on the headhunter's horizon — as far as he is concerned, they are generally bad news — but they nevertheless merit some consideration here, forming as they do a kind of lost tribe among whom many are well worth reclaiming. If, as is undoubtedly true, executive talent is in short supply, part of the answer is to be found in redeploying men who have received their corporate handshakes but have no wish to be put out to grass. The great problem is that employers tend to take the view (and they are by no means always wrong) that executives who have been made redundant must be well past their best and incapable of making a real contribution.

One can well understand, then, why headhunters fight shy of redundant executives. A client presented with a shortlist containing the names of one or two out of work executives is hardly likely to exclaim, "Well done, my good and faithful servant!" It may all be extremely shortsighted, but that is often the way of the marketplace, and a really formidable educational task would be needed to change this attitude.

One or two headhunters, on the other hand, will and do act for redundant executives at the special request of valued clients, though such help is often confined to counselling rather than going out on a limb to find jobs for such

131

individuals. One headhunter who offers a counselling service is Michael Wood, managing director of Search & Assessment Services of Banbury, who stressed that a lot of corporate "staff" jobs — in personnel, planning, research and special projects, for example — were being affected by the present recession, and so too were executives returning from overseas some of whom were finding "re-entry problems" at their home base.

Flexible approach

"Yet executive redundancy is not too much of a problem", he added, "because at this level it can be handled on an individual basis with plenty of flexibility on both sides. Moreover, a redundancy package consisting of a lump sum, reduced pension plus retention of the company car can add up to a very attractive deal, and in this way a chief executive can "structure" a redundancy, if he's so inclined."

Michael Wood also made the point that attitudes determining executive mobility had altered drastically in the ten years since the last big shake-out in 1971. "At that time", he said, "practically every redundant executive I spoke to was prepared to move house. Today it is all quite different. Most of them want and are determined to stay put."

All in all, Michael Wood summed up, the cost of an executive redundancy package may seem high, but in his opinion it could prove a bargain in the long run for any company wishing to get rid of an incompetent or unpopular executive while avoiding the expensive uncertainties of litigation. As part of the army of unemployed, of course, redundant executives are entitled, for what it is worth, to their full share of bleeding heart sympathy, but the reality is often quite different. No one need shed even crocodile tears over some "tragic victim of monetarism" heading for the golf course or car showroom with a five-figure handshake. The real priority is somehow to enable those with something to give to be in a position to give it. This requires a very different type of approach than that of the search or selection consultant, and an example of what can be done is looked at later in this chapter.

Meanwhile it should be borne in mind that executive redundancy is still relatively rare in the United Kingdom, even though it is today on the increase. At the same time, according to Theon Wilkinson, manager of the Employee Relations Department at the Institute of Personnel Management, "selective" or "convenience" redundancy at this level is still a fact of business life. "Moreover", he went on, "for many executives being made redundant is still a cause for shame. They feel it counts against them, especially in the sales field, when they're being interviewed for another job. The same rarely applies in the cases of blue-collar redundancy."

IPM view

The same point was brought out in a special IPM Information Report on *Executive Redundancy* published in 1980.

"Prospective employers", it stated, "not infrequently display some caution in regarding redundancy as a genuine reason for leaving an employer. In other words, it is not unknown for companies to disguise in the form of a redundancy what is in fact a ploy for getting rid of an unwanted executive."

Headhunters are well aware of this, and accordingly keep their distance. In a perfect world, of course, they would treat each redundant executive on his merits, but in the real world they just cannot spare the time.

"Redeployment" is a word often bandied about by people when discussing problems of executive redundancy, and in the large organisation or in the company which is part of a group there may indeed be opportunities to redeploy someone who has lost his job in another part of the empire. Here, too, however, companies often run up against problems of executive mobility, or the cut-back means that there are no jobs elsewhere in the organisation or, indeed, resources for re-training. For the older executive, on the other hand, it may be possible to find an "older statesman", semi-consultative type of niche, though this too may cause problems where there is a sharply-defined career structure and an organisation chart treated as holy writ.

On possibilities such as these, the I.P.M. report makes the following, slightly acid comment:

"It is always assumed that an executive would rather leave the organisation than accept a job with a lower grade or status. This may mean in fact that individuals are not given the choice. There is said to be a clear conviction, particularly among private sector employers, that a clean break is easier to accept than an unsatisfactory alternative. The cynical may well pose the question: easier for whom?"

According to Theon Wilkinson, however, an element of "after care" is beginning to show in the executive redundancy field, with one or two firms now using their personnel department resources in an attempt to find posts for staff they have had to let go. "In the past", he pointed out, "British firms have thought of redundancy primarily in terms of financial compensation. Now the continuing, supportive approach found widely throughout the E.E.C. is starting to come through here."

Headhunters' approach

One way in which this "supportive approach" occasionally finds practical expression is, as stated, through counselling of redundant executives by the client's headhunter. The following are some responses I received on this question from headhunters (they are quoted anonymously as in my opinion it is unfair to burden them with unsought and unpaid work):

"We have no counselling service as such, but sometimes we are asked to help by a client, and recently we bent over backward to help a former managing director client in trouble. This is very much a "casting one's bread upon the waters" type of activity."

"Yes, we do a little counselling on behalf of clients, and we do it free."

"As to acting for the redundant executive, the very positive answer is "No". We have considerable scepticism about the real quality of the service provided by "outplacement consultancies" (the current euphemism). Not to put too fine a point on it, our own view is that, with a few exceptions, much that is sold to the desperate, unemployed candidate is either incompetent or dishonest."

"We never act for the redundant executive; however, from time to time, clients do ask us to see executives whom they are declaring redundant. We only do this as a matter of courtesy, although we point out that there are very few ways other than in an advisory way in which we can help."

"No, we never act as outplacement agents, but we do counsel a client's redundant executives."

"We do devote time to counselling executives seeking jobs, but such time is limited and we make no charge."

The term "outplacement agency" is interesting, though why it should be used in preference to "executive employment agency" is not clear. At any rate, the above replies suggest that, although search and selection consultants are fairly unanimous about not acting for redundant executives, except as a special favour to clients, they are not absolutely unanimous on the matter. It is also interesting that most of them seem to make no charge for the service even though it must be fairly time-consuming.

Self-marketing

As matters stand at present, the "despised" outplacement agencies seem to form the main hope for the redundant executive, and in fact many personnel departments turn to such agencies as part of the redundancy "package". As with headhunters, their quality, integrity and approach can vary widely, but here we look in some detail at one of the most remarkable of such agencies — namely, that of Percy Coutts & Co Ltd of Grand Buildings, Trafalgar Square, W.C.2, which offers an Executive Redeployment Programme based on what the company's chairman, Tom Carew, has christened "executive self-marketing".

"This is very much a full-time occupation", Tom Carew assured me, "and the notion that a man without a job has nothing to do is quite disgraceful. There is in fact a job for every single one of my clients somewhere in the United Kingdom without my help, but my role is to improve the quality of the jobs they get and reduce the time it takes them to get a job."

Carew, whose business has offices in Manchester, Birmingham and Bath as well as in London, and a consulting staff of ten, points out that, with self-marketing, the redundant executive, or "client" in this case, more often than not obtains a job which did not exist previously. "After having taken our four-month Foundation Course", he claimed, "the majority of our clients create their own jobs. The crazy thing about it all is that people who come to us may have MBAs or any other qualifications and experience you care to think of. They have learned how to serve their chief executives and their businesses, but not one of them has had as much as an hour's training on how to market their skills and abilities to their own advantage."

"The term 'job hunting'," Carew continued, "implies that the candidate is looking for something which already exists, whereas with self-marketing he is creating his own market — often, indeed, an employer doesn't know he has a job for the right man."

Tom Carew also stresses that very often it is the job and not the man which is redundant, though he admits that most of the clients who come to his office — more than 80 per cent of them sent by their former employers — arrive very low in self-confidence. "But we teach them to act with confidence even though they don't feel it", he added, "and also not to act like puppets at a job interview. The fact is that most clients do not really have any problems, but they just can't market themselves."

The mechanics of the Coutts operation are contained within a four-month Foundation course, during which each client has his own tutor (or "housemaster") who stays with him until he has found a job. The course seeks primarily to develop self-marketing skills, but is reinforced by career counselling and by active help in setting up interviews with prospective employers. "Once we accept a client", Carew remarked, "we stay with him until he has found a job, and the average "stay" with us lasts 4.2 months. His consultancy fights shy of two main types: the executive who takes to the bottle and, in Carew's own words, "the six-figure handshake man who prefers the golf course." As noted, well over 80% of the clients are sponsored by their last employers, who include many well known names, starting with Shell in the early 1970s and today reading like a selection from *The Times* Top 1,000 companies. The fee for the service is 15% of the client's last salary, plus £500 if he is over 50. One remarkable feature of the whole operation, however, is that more than 10 per cent of clients pay their own fees.

There can be little doubt that Tom Carew, who holds a DSO and Croix de Guerre for service with the Resistance forces during the war, has very much stamped his own personality upon the service. He is a restless, quick thinking person, apparently full of self-confidence, who describes himself as "a Socratic person interested only in the individual". He seems to have a gift for injecting people with his own enthusiasms, and is convinced that most clients undervalue themselves in the initial stages of the "treatment". "But I am very much an opponent of the Peter Principle", he claims. "A lot of people are simply not aware of what they have to offer and because they've been made redundant they feel themselves to be in a state of sin. People assume that the last employer is always right and that the individual is in the wrong, while headhunters wouldn't make the slightest effort to locate and talk to a redundant executive. Yet I myself never take anyone on my consulting staff who hasn't had a hiccough in his career."

Carew is also firmly against his clients lowering their sights, as often happens with individuals who have received good severance terms and are content as a result to take something less than the job and the money they once had. "If the job is too small, good people get bored and do it badly", he insists, "and in any case employers don't buy "busted flushes" nor pay £12,000 to £25,000 people."

He supports this argument with actual case histories, one concerning a client who applied to a trade association in the food industry which happened to be advertising the post of marketing director. He did not specifically apply for that job but to discuss the industry and its problems. In the event, Carew claims, he came out of the interview with the job of chief executive at a salary of £16,000 compared with the £8,000 being offered for the marketing job. Another case concerned an executive with an engineering group who was sacked as a "poor performer" but, in Carew's opinion, the real reason was that he was superior to the work he had been given. "We told him to double his salary claim and to go after a job more in keeping with his skills and ability. In fact he got a job at double his previous money and today rates his own company aircraft, yet when he came to us that man had no belief in himself whatever."

As one would expect, Carew sees a tremendous need for the type of service he offers but claims that industrial society in general is not ready to accept what can be done in this field. His attitude to headhunters, moreover, rests very much this side of idolatry. "The whole headhunting attitude is repugnant to us", he claims, "though, like them, I've no time for concepts such as "rehabilitation" and "do-goodery", and in fact we provide our own people to headhunters for nothing. We produce a monthly *Executive Gazette* giving details of our clients to some 250 headhunters."

Response, it is claimed, is surprisingly good — about 150 requests for career histories within the first two to three days, after which a steady trickle. Which would seem to imply that search and selection men are not wholly insensitive to the possibilities of redundant executives. Like Shakespeare's toad, here and there one of them may contain a shining jewel in his head.

Changes in the air
The Percy Coutts executive redeployment programme has been dealt with here in some detail because of the

originality of the basic idea on which it rests. It is only fair to add, however, that there are numerous other consultancies which purport to help redundant executives, forming collectively a sector of the recruitment market in which survival is very much a function of effectiveness. In terms of scale of course, PER is the section leader, but this particular body depends on government support.

What emerges from all this, however, is that the redundant executive is no quarry for the headhunter, not at the moment anyway. But we do well to remember that headhunters themselves were unknown in this country some 25 years ago, and it looks as if the 1980s will be a decade of radical change in the recruitment industry as a whole. The portents are examined more closely in the final chapter.

11
Polishing the Image

An area of neglect

Far too much can be made of the BIM/IPM survey finding that only about 4% of companies ever use the services of search consultants and that only a further 14% use selection consultants. What really matters is that nearly all large and multi-national companies use headhunters, not to mention a growing number of small firms which have no other door on which to knock for the talent they are seeking. Here, in fact, we have a typical Pareto Distribution whereby less than 20% of firms provide well over 80% of the total market.

A much more basic and serious problem confronting search consultants is that of image improvement. Although some 25 years have passed since headhunters first set up shop in the United Kingdom, and although there can be no doubt that they are now being "accepted" more and more in the business and management world, suspicion and hostility remain concerning both their function and their integrity. As I have already argued, this is largely the fault of headhunters themselves. They tend to be suspicious of and "bitchy" about each other, and the British end of the profession at least has made no serious attempt to shape any kind of self-regulatory body which could both carry out public relations on behalf of British headhunters as a whole and see that its members adhere to an acceptable code of professional conduct.

141

MCA code

From this general criticism, I must except the Management Consultants Association of 23-24, Cornwall Place, London SW7, formed in 1956, which claims to be "the only association of established management consulting firms in the United Kingdom". The MCA lists only 25 members, albeit many of them leading names in the consultancy profession, and no headhunters as such. It cannot therefore claim to speak for the recruitment industry in Britain. On the other hand, some of its members offer search and selection within their scope of services, so the MCA Code of Professional Practice covering executive selection activities could serve as a foundation on which any new code could be built.

The MCA Code in question, to which members have to conform, specifies that consultants engaged in executive selection or search activities should possess "levels and standards of academic and professional competence approved by Council as appropriate." In addition, the Code sets out the consultant's obligations to clients and candidates, including the following:-

* Members will undertake only those assignments which they are competent to handle.

* They should confirm that the client has a genuine vacancy and that the terms and conditions of the position are suitable.

* Only candidates with suitable qualifications, background and experience will be put forward.

* Before the assignment begins, the consultants will confirm in writing the formal understanding regarding the type and calibre of person who is required. The letter will also contain details of the fees and other costs as well as terms

* In no case are fees for selection or search assignments

142

contingent on the placement of an executive.

* When undertaking executive search assignments, consultants will not approach employees of client companies on behalf of another client.

* As to obligations to candidates, members must be satisfied that the job is a viable one and that a genuine vacancy exists.

* The advantages and disadvantages of the job must be objectively portrayed.

* The anonymity of candidates must be preserved unless specific permission is given to disclose this information.

* The candidate must be informed when no longer under consideration and at least within one month of the job being filled or the assignment terminated.

It may be rightly objected that much of this is pure window-dressing, but the point is surely that window-dressing is a necessary ingredient in most business activities. If the headhunting profession is known and seen to operate a strict code of practice — no matter how often such a code may be covertly ignored or neglected — nothing is more likely to raise or at least maintain the prestige of the activity in the eyes of industry, commerce and government alike. At present, however, because of the secrecy which must shroud the headhunter's job, it is all too easy for the prospective client to gain an impression of furtiveness, of grey men skulking through the marketplace, the "spies" of whom MacKenzie Davey has written.

What about rights?
Enough, then, of the headhunter's obligations. Has this much-maligned creature no rights, this man to whom many a leading company the world over has turned when in trouble?

143

The answer is "Yes, of course the headhunter has rights, but here again it is up to him to stand up confidently and proclaim these." No one else is going to do the job for him.

The client's obligations to the headhunter have already been discussed, including the latter's right to as much relevant information about the company to do his job properly. He has a right to know something of the client's future plans and to savour the managerial "chemistry", and also to expect that the client will prove reasonably flexible over matters of salary and fringe benefit. And the headhunter has a right to know especially where he is being used to supply a makeweight shortlist, including a named candidate whom the client has already chosen for the job. "This happens from time to time", I was told by a leading headhunter in London's West End, "and of course we are well aware of it when it happens. The fun begins if we come up with a candidate who is in every way better than the person the client had in mind."

The headhunter's rights as far as candidates or (in the case of selection consultants) applicants are concerned are more difficult to pinpoint, for the candidate or applicant tends as a rule to react to moves by the other two in the triangle. Punctuality, politeness and the right to be informed if there is a change in the candidate's circumstances or attitude to the job are what a headhunter may reasonably expect from this side of the line. "Frivolous" interest on the part of candidates is by no means unknown, especially in the course of a search assignment. "I can well understand this reaction", I was told by the editor of a leading industrial publication who was headhunted for the post. "In my own case, my first reaction was one of immense gratification. I felt both surprised and flattered in the extreme, and then I began to be intrigued as to how they have gone along with it all just to satisfy my curiosity about these points, though of course I was delighted to be offered the job."

Headhunters free to choose

Returning to the client-consultant relationship, it is worth making the point that the headhunter may choose his clients with the same freedom as the client appoints a headhunter. True, in today's circumstances, headhunters do not turn down many assignments, but the more successful of them are able to do so, and I have no doubt that the profession as a whole will become increasingly selective as its influence and scale of operations grows.

To give one example. In his book, *Secrets of a Corporate Headhunter*, John Wareham advises fellow members of his profession: "However hungry you may be, the courage to walk away from some prospects is the key to building a stable of satisfied clients. In the final analysis, the quality of your base list of prospects reflects your own personality, the quality of your service and your future." John Wareham then lists the types of client for whom his own consultancy will not act. These are based on the following criteria:-

"We don't accept an assignment for a corporation unless it is providing a valuable service for the community. It's not that we are idealists, just that it's difficult to recruit good executives for questionable clients."

"We don't recruit for corporations that are dying. Some quite large international corporations are held together by creditors and rubber bands."

"We don't accept assignments from clients who want to pretend that we are paid employees. I turned down a major corporation in New York that wanted to both supervise us and assign some of their own staff to actually work alongside us — and using *our* name . . ."

"We don't need clients who expect us to agree with all their foibles and prejudices."

"I am wary of a prospect who tells me he has used everyone else in town without success."

"I don't like a client who denigrates his entire executive team."

These are some of the "prejudices" culled from the experience of one of the world's most successful headhunters,

145

and I have no doubt that many other people in this branch of the recruitment profession will at least agree with them in secret, however much their business pressures may force them to swallow their pride. There is no doubt that some of the leading British headhunters have by now established a relationship with clients based on equality (and perhaps even fraternity) into which, if need be, a take-it-or-leave-it element may operate. "Ideally, of course", said David Blamey of Spencer Stuart, "the client can help by trusting the consultant, and this is a two-way process. In the main, problems arise through lack of mutual respect and understanding between client and consultant. Very large companies produce communication difficulties. Very small ones sometimes are tempted to recruit "big company people" who may be expert but are ineffective in such a different environment."

Polishing the headhunting image, then, depends very largely on a better understanding between headhunter and client, a state of affairs, which cannot be assumed to follow automatically from the placing of even a successful assignment in the hands of a consultant. There do not seem to be so many problems on the candidate side, the majority of whom undoubtedly enjoy being "searched". The most delicate problem here of course is that of letting the unsuccessful candidate down as gently as possible after having allowed his hopes to soar.

PR priority

A high standard of business morality, one which is seen to exist and to apply widely, is then a *sine qua non* for the headhunting profession if it is to realise its full potential. Yet this of itself is not enough. This part of the recruitment industry must also radically improve its public relations; in fact, it must introduce a public relations facility.

The headhunting industry in Britain has so far failed to do this, in my view, because of the intense suspicions and jealousies to be found still among existing consultancies. It was the American writer, H.L. Mencken, who described a puritan as "someone haunted by the fear that somewhere someone is having a good time." Paraphrasing this delightful thought, I would describe quite a lot of British headhunters as people haunted by the fear that somewhere, some competitor is stealing a march on them. Perhaps it is partly because confidentiality is one of the badges of the activity, and maybe another reason is that the search industry has had to contend with a lot of hostility from business and management circles, leading perhaps to feelings of guilt. I tend, however, to the more simplistic explanation that competition for clients among headhunters has been too cut-throat, and rewards for the successful too easy, for any unifying tendencies to have taken hold. The search part of the industry has, as it were, become a victim of its own secretiveness.

Yet there can be no doubt that the industry urgently needs to set up an Association (or Society or Executive or Council or whatever) to direct its affairs and handle its public relations at that level. There already is an Association of Executive Search Consultants somewhere, I am told, though most headhunters I have spoken to about it seem to think that it is "more or less defunct". Be that as it may, the industry ought to be considering as a number one priority the setting up of a body to put across the key message that headhunting is a legal and useful service (which in fact it is) and certainly no more immoral than other forms of recruitment, talent scouting for soccer teams included. Another key PR function of such a body should consist of the regular issue of material for press, radio and TV giving estimated figures of turnover for the industry and details of new trends and techniques. At the moment, headhunting firms do receive quite a lot of random publicity in business and consumer magazines, mainly because of the human interest element which pervades the activity, but we hear and see little or nothing about trends within the industry as a whole. How many businessmen realise, for example, that search properly carried out is a highly cost effective service?

One headhunter who is passionately convinced of the

need for the search industry to market itself is Ferry Ward, then of Brook Street Executive Resources. "I see four main ways of improving business", he said. "First, there is word of mouth recommendation, and there is nothing better than that but it has to be earned. Secondly, headhunters should make every recruitment advertisement they place a corporate advertisement as well. The copy should be distinctive, specific, informative and readable, and its general design should make the reader aware of the company who inserted it. Thirdly, there is editorial coverage through PR activities, often an area of utter neglect, and lastly there is the hard, personal sell approach, by telephone initially — I'm not very good at this myself but it's often where the profit lies."

Above all, however, the industry must first grow in confidence and rid itself of its petty guilts and suspicions. If it can do this, then its future, as already argued, is set fair.

12
The Way Ahead

Small stays beautiful

Only greed or stupidity can prevent the headhunting industry from going from strength to strength in the foreseeable future, for the simple reason that talented people are needed more and more in today's world. "The age of machines" may not be a meaningless phrase, but fantasies of a world being taken over by computers and robots are, at best, amiable nonsense; only when objects made by man can acquire the capacity for making value judgements and for recreating themselves need the human race begin to worry on that score. Meanwhile, it can be easily demonstrated that, in a world of declining standards, real human talent is going to be needed more than ever. The headhunters, then, are batting on a good wicket, provided they do not try to hit against the spin.

The quest for executive talent may of course affect the structure of the search and selection industry in a number of ways, but it is likely to remain true to the notion that "small is beautiful". Headhunting firms may now span the globe with their networks of offices in the major commercial centres of the five continents. The individual unit, however, has remained of modest size; Korn/Ferry International, for example, thought to be the largest executive search business in the world, has 26 offices and 250 consultants.

149

"It's got to be this way", commented Alan Cotton, head of executive recruitment at the MLH Consulting Group, "in order to keep the business personal and intimate. The farther you get away from this, the closer you get to treating people as units. Executive recruitment is a story about people, people, people — it is not and never will be a quantifiable business."

Where the recruitment industry may witness a fundamental change over the next few years, however, is in the interaction between selection and search. As noted at the beginning, the selection approach uses the trawl whereas the search man uses a line with a carefully baited hook, but the difference is not quite as straightforward as this metaphor would suggest. On the selection side, there is always the problem of creating a daunting pile of administrative work with each assignment and perhaps of not attracting anyone really suitable in the process: with search, on the other hand, the more a particular market is worked, the more stale and incestuous it becomes, with the consequent danger of headhunters ending up chasing their own tails, so to speak.

There is also the problem of a dwindling cost gap between the two methods, created by the soaring cost of advertising — and this is a cost which is likely to keep on going up and up. I have already pointed out that this trend is bringing the cost of a selection assignment often in line with that of a search job, and this could well influence a client to go for the "more prestigious" search option. But not always, as is underlined by the following case history recounted by Alan Cotton.

"This was a recent assignment in which we were asked to recruit an executive president for a large international organisation at a salary of $150,000 and the total package worth about $200,000. The client suggested that we could find a suitable person through search techniques, but he was seeking "freshness" so I thought it would be best to cast a wider net and decided on selection (our business uses both techniques)."

"We advertised in three publications — *The Wall Street Journal, The Financial Times* and *The Sunday Times* — expecting a total of between 350 and 400 replies. In the event, we got 706 replies from all over the world — much to the benefit of my wife's stamp album — and the interesting thing was that we got replies not only from scions of industry but also from ambassadors, generals, admirals and top civil servants. In the end we managed to reduce the response to a "shortlist" of 20, but the point is that we couldn't have achieved the same breadth of response from search techniques."

At the same time, Cotton agreed that the cost of recruitment advertisements was becoming "horrendous", pointing out that at national press level the cost per response was now over £30 in many cases. "Yet it still justifies the advertisement as a means of attracting people where the field is wide enough", he commented.

Search, by contrast, comes into its own not only with top executive posts calling for specific areas of technology. "We had one case", Bert Young of Alexander Hughes & Associates pointed out, "where we were asked to find a specialist in fluid bed catalysts for a leading chemical company, and at the end of our search we discovered that there were only eight people in the world with the necessary experience and qualifications."

The selection approach could not have dealt with this assignment.

My own view is that, on balance, the soaring cost of advertising vacancies (which is paid by the client of course) will slowly squeeze business towards the search consultancies. I wholly agree that selection always offers the possibility of a high flyer coming through the window, as it were, but in the end it boils down to whether the client is looking for Superman or simply the best available. Very, very occasionally, the selection approach will discover some rare talent and often it will unearth someone who is more than adequate for the post in question. A search consultancy, on the other hand, will claim to find the best available person. Neither process need take significantly longer than the other, and the client is often faced with a finely balanced choice. More often than not, of course, he will ignore both courses of action and plump for doing his own advertising and selecting, as indeed is the case with the substantial majority of employers.

As I have said, however, I think commerce and industry over the next few years will tend to lean more towards search than selection techniques. Despite the suspicion in which headhunting is still held, many more employers and candidates are impressed by this activity than would openly admit to it. For some, it carries a whiff of daring and ruthlessness, even of wickedness. Truly it has been said that there's nowt as queer as folk.

The industry's crystal ball
But how does the headhunting industry see its own future? Over a large area of the activity, it seems to be very much a matter of "so many men, as many opinions", though it would be a weird industry in which members were unanimous on every point. Indeed, no sooner had I finished Chapter Ten, in which I allege that redundant executives are bad news to headhunters, than I met a selection consultant who regards them as an invaluable source of talent and experience − so much so in fact that he gives certain redundant executives from his files advance notice of when he is going to advertise certain vacancies for which, in his opinion, they are suitable, and he invites them to apply along with other applicants. The most we can really hope for, then, is a prevailing view.

To this end, I invited a number of leading United Kingdom headhunters to give me their views on how they saw the future of the recruitment industry, and in particular the search part of it, developing. A selection of replies is printed below so that readers can form their own views.

First of all, the view of a specialist headhunter (in publishing),

Roger Stacey of Astron Appointments Ltd.
"I hope the headhunter will tend to specialise; otherwise, except for the very top jobs (e.g. the head of British Steel) he will in my view himself become redundant. If specialisation increases, I would expect as a logical outcome to see more, but smaller, firms appearing; and those firms to be organised vertically, as Astron is, and able to cope with recruitment at all levels within a given sphere of activity. . . I do think that there will be increasing pressure towards licensing, which is already necessary for firms such as ourselves."

Peter Chalkley, managing director of Sabre International Search, London, SW1.
"The industry will grow rapidly for a number of reasons. First, the soaring cost of advertising plus the time involved in sifting and assessing replies and interviewing, is making search more and more competitive. Secondly, there is the increasingly confidential nature of the technology-based industries; firms are putting a screen round their future plans. Third, there has been the failure of our education system and lack of good management development, so that talent is scarce and has to be searched. In our experience, good people stand out like beacons. Fourth is the increasing use of headhunters by government departments, though I'm sad to see our own Government using so many U.S. firms."

Anthony Langdon, chairman, Eurosurvey Ltd.
"In Europe, the market for search is buoyant and growing steadily. After 22 years, clients in this part of the world are beginning to use headhunters as they would a lawyer or merchant banker. We are becoming highly respected as a profession."

Christopher Wysock-Wright, chairman, Wrightson Wood.
"I am very optimistic. I see the headhunting firm becoming the client's most important outside adviser, and in ten

years' time you'll find headhunters, like merchant bankers, on the boards of many important companies, and we'll also be more involved in the work and needs of government departments. We will be involved more and more in the high technology recruiting field — and, indeed, in every level of appointment where our service can be shown to be cost effective."

David Blamey of Spencer Stuart Management Consultants. "We will become more widely involved in the whole management development and team building sense. There will be specialists also and new firms will certainly emerge. Government departments will make increasing use of us and stricter licensing will probably follow."

Nigel Rugman, director of Management Appointments, London, W1.
"Specialisation and close, continuing relationships with client companies are, in our view, the best basis for long-term success. Clearly, any legislation which limits the activities of "cowboys" is a good thing, although there is little evidence that the Employment Agencies Act, for example, has done anything in this regard. Unless the next Socialist government is made up of the idiot fringe of the Labour Party, there is no reason to suppose that the role of the private recruitment consultancy will not continue."

R.A.B. Gowlland, managing partner, Egon Zehnder International (one of the largest search firms with a turnover thought to be in the region of $17 million)
"Like any consultancy firm, I believe that in the 1980s executive search will become more specialised, and we are currently considering how we can best adapt to this trend. Undoubtedly more executive search firms will appear on the scene. However, there will be a large number of mergers and many firms will also go to the wall, particularly small locally-based firms. The net result will be a concentration

of the work in the hands of the few professional, international firms."

"Government departments will also make increasing use of the services of firms in the executive search field. Certainly if a Socialist government is elected, there will be increasing pressure towards more onerous licensing regulations."

Garry Long of Management Selection Limited.

"Yes, government will certainly make greater use of headhunters because it is the best way of getting the best men. I don't think the actual size of the industry will increase, however, though more specialisation is inevitable. As regards licensing, I think the top end of the industry is more likely to respond to professional discipline than to legislation — after all, the original legislation in this field was designed to protect domestic servants and actors. But as long as fees are payable by the client, and the whole operation is backed by professional standards, there is no need for legislation. As for "poaching", legislation can do nothing about that, but in an open market it is self-defeating in the long run."

John Reid, managing director, Executive Search Ltd.

"The market for the search consultant will expand, though there are disadvantages to specialisation. We hope government departments will make more use of our services. Some of the appointments for which they have been responsible have been questionable, to say the least. We are already licensed, and if attempts are made to curtail our clients, and our freedom, ways will be found to re-establish it."

Bert Young of Alexander Hughes & Associates.

"I see two main influences on the future of our industry. First, the main consultancies will continue with the existing market, though specialists may mushroom. Secondly, government departments will make more and more use of us."

From all this it would seem that the search and selection industry is more or less unanimous that government use of its services is going to grow steadily throughout the 1980s, also that more specialisms will develop within the field, which in turn will mean more consultancies. I think, however, that R.A.B. Gowlland is right when he says that the market will be dominated more and more by a few international, professional firms, although I do not share the implication that headhunters have to be big and international in order to be professional.

A political threat?
Again, as a tribe, headhunters do not seem to be too worried about the possibility of a far-Left Socialist Government coming to power, an attitude which, in my opinion, betrays a certain degree of complacency. Of course there are sound economic reasons for leaving the recruitment industry free to work out its own destiny, and obviously its activities could benefit a Labour-directed economy just as effectively as a free enterprise economy.

Specialists?
More specialisation within the headhunting field seems, by common agreement, to be a likely trend during the 1980s, with target areas such as high technology of every description — computing, offshore exploration, nuclear power, civil engineering and the like — transport and freighting, and financial management (in which already quite a number of headhunters are beginning to look for people who have what it takes to be general managers). Mike Millington of Fleet Personnel Selection — "we're interested wherever cargo is managed" — claims that the "wide experience" of the non-specialist is the main reason why sometimes they are not as effective as the specialist (sic). "Variety of work", he maintains, "deprives them of the time to keep up with developments in a specific market."

That may well be true, but the headhunter seeking the really top assignments, and who hopes to maintain an "international dimension" to his activities, has to be something of a generalist. There is nothing to prevent his acquiring a specialisation into the bargain, but it is somehow fitting to the cause of headhunting as a whole that its practitioners be seen as men for all seasons. The market at present is big enough to accommodate both types of service, though increasing specialisation is a sign of the times, and Mike Millington is probably right when he advises potential recruiters; "if you're starting up today, choose something specific and stay with it."

The overall balance in the recruitment industry between generalist and specialist is not likely to be greatly disturbed, however, by the arrival of more specialists on the scene, and in any case the top international headhunting consultancies would undoubtedly fight back vigorously if the specialists began to acquire too much of the market, primarily by forming specialist divisions themselves.

Another development anticipated by quite a number of established search and selection consultants is the arrival upon the scene of redundant executives armed with five-figure handshakes and the conviction that a career in consultancy beckons. Something along these lines is bound to happen, in my view, if only because for some years now redundant executives have gravitated to sundry forms of consultancy like ducks to the proverbial pond. In the process, consciously or otherwise, they could add to the "cowboy" population within the industry.

"As people in senior executive positions are made redundant while they still have something to give", Alan Cotton stated, "some will undoubtedly gravitate into the recruitment industry. There are a number of cowboys of course, as in any service industry, so the rest of us have to protect our reputation in terms of satisfied candidates as well as clients. On balance, satisfying the candidate is even more important because he represents the client's profitable future. Consider that, over a 20-year period, the client could be investing as much as £1 million in a candidate we or some other consultancy found for him. That is the onus which rests on our industry."

There is of course, no reason why redundant executives should not bring a sense of integrity and responsibility to a career in head-hunting, not to mention also a flair for the activity, but the industry has been established long enough to be wary of newcomers, although in fact it has been in existence in the United Kingdom for a mere 25 years.

Again, setting up as a headhunter is by no means as simple as it may sound. According to Christopher Wysock-Wright, there are four main hurdles to be negotiated before any such business can get off the ground. These are:-

1. The newcomer has to be known as an individual in business circles.
2. He has to have clients prepared to use his services.
3. The cash flow has to be there from the beginning — which means billing at the end of every month.
4. Most difficult of all, he has to get a team together with the right blend of skills and experience.

None of these tasks is obviously going to be easy for the redundant executive whose business contacts are likely to be confined to a relatively narrow area of industry or commerce.

Yet I doubt whether problems such as these — which are common to quite a number of businesses — will deter the really determined executive, who will have heard, and it is true, that the rate of profit from successful headhunting can be highly gratifying.

Functional changes
As to whether there will be a major shift in fuction among headhunters from search consultant pure and simple, (figuratively speaking, of course) to search consultant cum management developer, much may depend on events taking place at the top of the search tree in the U.S.A. There, after a golden decade, the leading search firms, notably the Big Six, are finding that their hunting grounds are beginning to shrink, forcing them in turn to look twice at the two-year

off-limits rule approved by the Association of Executive Recruiting Consultants, a much more virile and influential body than its British counterpart. Clients naturally liked this rule because it gave them two years' grace from personnel raids by their own search consultants, though of course it still left them vulnerable to the depredations of other headhunters. For their part, the Big Six think the rule should be softened or fudged, not in order to keep growing, it is claimed, but to keep them from shrinking, and they point to the "unethical" practice of some client firms of throwing them a middle-level, pot-boiler of an assignment every two years in order to keep the off-limits rule in full working order.

Some of the Big Six companies are contemplating treating a client's various divisions as separate businesses in order to get round the rule. Recently, however, Lester Korn of Korn/Ferry International, the world's largest search company, decided that the only solution for the large companies in the long run was to go vertical — that is, to do more business with fewer clients by encouraging the latter to use their headhunters to search not only chief and top executives but others lower down the ladder. Following this decision, it is reported that one Korn Ferry partner has been assigned to each client both to drum up business and to act as a human resources adviser. Other members of the Big Six, it seems, are sticking to their traditional policies in the meantime, but business experts expect that in time they will follow the Korn/Ferry lead — as the only means of achieving revenue growth without steady expansion of the client list.

Headhunting came to Britain from the U.S.A. and so did a number of its subsequent refinements, so it is reasonable to assume that if "going vertical" catches on to a large extent across the Atlantic, then it will come to these shores in due course. In which case a number of leading consultants in our own headhunting firms would become "human resources advisers", and that in my view is basically a more attractive term than "management developer".

Already we can see an initial movement along this path in the fact that an increasingly large part of the revenue of British search firms now comes from repeat business.

It may of course be objected that progress towards the status of human resources adviser is likely to be much slower in Britain than in the U.S.A. because of the non-cooperative attitude of personnel departments in this country, though I think "lukewarm" would be a much fairer description. True, there is a much more cooperative attitude between American headhunters and company personnel executives than is found here, so training the two factions to live together for the common benefit of the company could be quite a challenge. Yet there should be no problem with small companies (quite a number of which go to headhunters when they need a good man) without any personnel department as such. As for the large corporation, a human resources adviser to the main board need not and should not be a thorn in the flesh of the head of personnel. The jobs in fact should be complementary, one presenting the market view and the other ensuring that corporate needs and policy are met.

As for the specialist head-hunter, there is no reason why he should not act as a manpower adviser as well as talent scout for the client with specific requirements. Companies which are constantly on the look-out for high quality specialists can and do profit from on-going relationships with specialist search consultancies.

Another force for change has been the recent move by one or two leading headhunters into recruiting non-executive directors for large companies. No one can say where this development will eventually lead, but it certainly marks a departure into fresh woods and pastures new, and as such is likely to be good for the recruitment industry.

The wind of change, then, is blowing through the headhunter's territory, as far as relations with clients are concerned. One area not yet considered, however, is that covering the personal circumstances of candidates and the very real problems of housing, children's education, of wives reluctant to live north of Watford and of executives reluctant to be promoted overseas in case of "re-entry difficulties". Not wishing to live anywhere outside the Home Counties may seem a trivial reason for turning down a good career opportunity, but any headhunter will confirm that it crops up often enough.

Other problems are founded in much more practical values. An acquaintance of mine, for example, was recently headhunted for quite a big publishing job in London, which meant his having to leave the Midlands with his wife and family and settle in a semi-fashionable district of the capital just south of the Thames. For his house in the Midlands, a four-bedroom semi, he received about £30,000 but has had to pay £68,000 for a similar property in the district where he now lives. His wife, meanwhile, had to give up her teaching job in the Midlands, and is bored and jobless in her new surroundings. I have no doubt that my friend has made the right decision, taking the long-term view — and he can afford to do so for he is still a young man — but who could blame an older executive with his children well established in some local school for turning down such an offer, even though it meant a salary almost treble what he was getting?

The common experience of search and selection men alike is that factors such as those mentioned have very little influence where really top jobs are involved — and, indeed, that is what one would expect. "At top level difficulties in moving home are rarely insuperable", commented R.A.B. Gowlland of Egon Zehnder, "but it tends to be a deterrent when children are being educated through the State system rather than the private system, but there are obviously a higher proportion of senior executives who use the latter." Or another view, this time from Roger Stacey of Astron Appointments Ltd: "We notice that with younger people the spouse's income is as important as their own, and therefore they cannot move unless two new jobs are potentially available. With somewhat older candidates, their children's education is, understandably, vitally important, especially as it is now not easy to find satisfactory

161

schools anywhere. There is also even the problem of aged parents, which can prevent some candidates from being able to move."

Most members of the recruitment profession agree that problems created by housing and children's education can make a decision to move very difficult indeed, and they also agree that the recession has made things worse, but they also share the view that such problems are not insuperable and that really outstanding candidates will find a way around these. "Especially", added Nigel Rugman, "where an intelligent employer is prepared to accept the full burden of relocation costs."

An interesting aspect of this topic is that there seems to be little difficulty in persuading British executives to take jobs overseas, where, as a rule, they seem to be much more highly thought of than at home. Perhaps they are better able to show their mettle in the freer business atmosphere abroad without any trade union albatross round their necks. One dissenting voice is that of John Reid of Executive Search Ltd who alleged that many British executives were taking jobs abroad because they were unemployable at home and that their quality was often "lamentable". Be that as it may, one reason why British executives seem quite prepared to take overseas jobs is undoubtedly that, oddly enough, the degree of domestic disruption is not nearly as severe in most cases as when changing jobs in the United Kingdom.

It is unlikely that any of the factors mentioned will change much over the next few years. Perhaps employers will become a bit more generous over relocation expenses — many already are — but the same problems of housing, children's education and not wanting to live north of Watford are not likely to alter much in the foreseeable future. Meanwhile, according to American headhunter, John Stork, whose consultancy has offices in London, Paris, Frankfurt and Amsterdam, British businessmen have a higher level of what he calls "perceived honesty" than most Europeans and they travel well. This, he thinks, may be a legacy from our imperial tradition, from the days when mad dogs and Englishmen went out in the noon-day sun. It is at least an interesting theory.

The money side

Headhunting fees will of course increase with inflation, though it is unlikely that there will be any radical changes in the way fees are structured. Some search consultants, perhaps an increasing number, will assess the assignment and charge a straight fee based on the degree of difficulty, status of the appointment and the time likely to be spent on the search. Special cases often attract special fees; for instance, Russell Reynolds were reportedly paid $700,000 for recruiting Ian MacGregor from an American investment bank to become chairman of the British Steel Corporation. The Swiss-based firm, Consultex SA, in its 1980 survey of the European search industry, noted that firms willing to work on a full or part contingency basis were still the exception, but it added that "basing at least part of the fee on the success of the search is a trend that is growing". Consultex commented that this can be an important factor in how much a company has to pay for search services "since, typically, only 70% of all search assignments result in a candidate being hired."

The increasing contingency element in fee-charging does not seem to be creating much of a furore in Western Europe, though, as noted, it is severely frowned upon by the leading headhunters in the United Kingdom. It is of course easy to see how a contingency arrangement can sour relations between headhunter and client and lead to accusations of "cowboy" and worse, but I have already argued that the main danger lies in the weak client who will not say "No" or haggle over the terms of such an assignment. Payment whether or not the search is successful may be a more gentlemanly procedure, but the client who misses out is hardly all searches are successful. To be fair to headhunters, however, many of them will not give up until they have found the right person, and more and more of them will find a replacement free of charge where a candidate of theirs has fallen down on the job.

When all's said and done, however, most headhunters are likely to continue charging between 25-35% of salary quoted, plus expenses, with the rate going up to perhaps 40% in special cases. At this rate, a good headhunter can make a very nice living indeed, and he would be a fool to risk it by deciding to charge more.

As for selection consultants and specialist search men, (whose method of operating is more akin to selection in any case) it is likely that the soaring cost of advertising will act as a brake on other elements contributing towards total fees. Print and publishing costs, though still just about tolerable, are rising faster than other types of costs in the recruiting market, and if the trend continues (as it undoubtedly will) it will give a keen competitive edge to the search men — or at least to those of them who never or only rarely advertise. The "£30 per response" quoted by Alan Cotton may represent value for money in a high quality field for a really top post, but it does not look or sound too healthy when linked to a middle management vacancy.

European brief

As we have seen, the search and selection industry is flourishing in North America, in Britain and Western Europe, in the Middle and Far East (largely through the operations of the international firms) and to a lesser degree in Africa and Latin America. I think, however, it may be worth keeping a special watch on developments in Western Europe where headhunting activities seem to be generating a great deal of interest. True, only a few months ago unemployment in the European Economic Community reached the the 10 million mark, but it is now clear that recession and large numbers out of work have little effect on activity in the upper reaches of the recruitment industry. It could be said in fact that the higher productivity and lower unit costs being achieved through cutting labour forces have in turn created a demand for skilled managers to maintain this new found efficiency.

Anyhow, figures published by Consultex and Eurosurvey Ltd both confirm that headhunting is the major management growth area of Western Europe. For his part, John Stork says that this is largely due to the multi-national companies such as Ford, Unilever, Royal Dutch Shell and the like, and in particular to the major American international groups, who have ever been on the look out for executive talent. However, what has happened since Britain joined the Common Market, says Stork, has been the emergence of European professional executives with the same highly paid mobility as their counterparts in the U.S.A. Moreover, the abolition of work permits and other national constraints within the EEC, have transformed executive opportunities in this part of the world, and today the European businessman "can hold up his credit card anywhere".

One effect of all this has been that the American multinational companies operating in Europe are looking for locally born executive talent to head their operations in the countries concerned. Finding such talent has meant good business for the headhunters of London, Paris, Brussels, Amsterdam, Zurich, Frankfurt and elsewhere. This, despite certain restrictions such as in France, where in theory recruitment is a State monopoly, though the laws relating to search firms are not strictly applied. Again, in West Germany, it is illegal to keep unauthorised personnel files or to contact prospective candidates for jobs without first placing a job advertisement in the press. "But", as one British headhunter remarked to me, "you will never stop people consulting."

As I see it, then, the growing level of headhunting activity in Western Europe will come to reflect a harsh economic truth — namely, that even if a recovery in output and trading takes place, it will do little to create jobs at the unskilled and semi-skilled end of the employment spectrum, whereas it will intensify the demand for the services of those whose skills and experience can make a positive contribution to controlling production costs and thereby increasing profits. It is a dangerous state of mind, in my opinion, to assume that an economic upturn will automatically solve problems of unemployment: the headhunters, by contrast, would appear to have a market whatever happens.

It has also been the experience of headhunters such as Eurosurvey Ltd that the main thrust of demand in Western Europe is directed at executives who can make a practical contribution rather than at management "intellectuals" such as planners. Production and financial experts are wanted almost everywhere, but there is also a brisk demand for expertise in tax law, biological and chemical processes and in the application of plastics technology.

Recruiting by advertisement

This would seem to be in keeping with the experience of job advertisement agencies in Britain and elsewhere, which form an extremely important limb of the headhunting industry today. At one such, Grey Advertising Ltd of Great Portland Street, London, W1, I was told by account executive Vivienne Borrie, that "headhunting is coming down more and more to the proletarian type of position, to the HNC or HND type of job. In our experience, engineers are wanted just as much as managers, and countries in Europe and elsewhere are beginning to come to Britain for them. This is possibly because we have a very comprehensive trade publications network in this country. At national level, meanwhile, the bulk of middle management jobs are advertised in *The Daily Telegraph*, but *The Daily Express*, with its northern and southern editions, is a favourite for engineering vacancies."

Vivienne Borrie shares the widely held view of the recruitment industry that every vacancy advertisement should also be a corporate advertisement, and she pointed out that this was particularly true of an agency such as hers which had to deal with clients operating on a strict budget and with no experience of marketing and recruiting. "We can offer an additional service", she continued, "including box numbers, interviewing facilities and an interviewing service, shortlisting and of course complete confidentiality. Some major agencies in fact employ a resident selection consultant, which naturally is not liked by the headhunters."

A recruitment advertisement, Vivienne Borrie stressed, should always promote the company image, presenting a picture of solidity, good prospects, interesting work. The job itself should be fully described, including duties and to whom the person appointed will be responsible and who will be responsible to him. So also should be the human requirements: qualifications, experience and personal attributes. Lastly, the job benefits and package: salary, relocation help, prospects, health insurance (if any), profit sharing cheap mortgages, company car etc.

With advertisement recruitment agencies, the selection process is basically a function of the advertisement, while the reverse is true of the selection consultancy. It looks as if the two are gradually moving closer in approach, and may one day become almost indistinguishable. As long as advertising in the local and national press remains the most popular way of seeking executive talent, one must expect advertisement agencies operating in this sector to keep on thinking of ways of improving their service, and this is a trend which no headhunter can afford to ignore.

Some headhunters of course, among them Sir John Trelawny of Korn/Ferry's London office, claim that the weakness of advertising, where middle and top management vacancies are concerned, is that it reaches only those who are active job seekers or dissatisfied with their existing jobs or the unemployed, and that therefore the odds against an advertisement reaching the ideal candidate are long indeed. But whether or not really talented people do scan the jobs pages is a matter of dispute. For his part, Alan Cotton maintains that a person who is actively looking for a better job is, *per se*, much better motivated than the executive who has to be enticed out of a comfortable rut. Yet another view is that senior executives are now expecting to be approached by headhunters and wondering whether they are losing their grip if the telephone does not ring.

Tot homines, quot sententiae!

Use him efficiently

During the present decade, for reasons already made clear, many organisations will be using headhunters for the first time, so it will behove them to make the best use of their money, i.e. to make the best use of the kind of service executive search and selection can provide. We have seen that, at its best, this service can offer confidentiality, objectivity, thoroughness and a professional approach, and that there is a considerable saving of top management time after the job specification has been agreed. The disadvantages of headhunting stem from unnecessary or inefficient use on the part of the client or from poor selection, often expressed in escalating costs or in inept handling of consultants – for instance, lack of frankness over the reasons for the vacancy or expecting too much for too little.

As to choosing a headhunter, firms new to the activity can always ask around; in this market, as elsewhere, nothing beats word-of-mouth recommendation. Advice is also available from the Management Consultants Association, but in any case potential clients may well be approached directly by telephone by headhunters themselves. There is nothing wrong in this of course; on the contrary, people who are adept at this form of cold calling may well be the type of people a client needs in order to achieve a successful placement. A fourth avenue of contact consists of articles by headhunters in the business and management press or in approaches at conferences and other types of business meetings. The thing always to bear in mind is that, although he is no superman, the search or selection consultant is a professional, and this in the final analysis is what the client pays for. His sources of information range from press cuttings, professional directories and membership lists to data supplied by special contacts within given industries and business sectors, plus the knowledge and contacts he has acquired for himself from years of simply doing the job. This, basically, is the headhunter's stock in trade whether or not he stores this knowledge on computers, card index systems or simply keeps most of it in his head.

At the same time, any search or selection consultant must be given certain relevant information by the client, if his services are to be properly exploited. Such information is most usefully summarised in BIM's *Management Information Sheet* No. 55 on "Using Executive Search Consultants". Though published in 1976, much of this document is relevant to the headhunting industry of today. Headhunters, it says, have the right to know about:-

* why the job became vacant;
* if new, why did the post become necessary;
* reasons for no inside promotion;
* place of job in the management structure;
* the proposed working relationship with subordinates and superiors;
* overall responsibilities of the post in question;
* company's past history and future plans;
* salary and benefits offered;
* time scale for the assignment;
* expenses — these should be agreed in advance;
* name of person in client company with whom consultant will be dealing;
* degree of confidentiality hedging the assignment; and
* what course of action is to be followed if, after the appointment, either the client or the successful candidate is unhappy.

The first two points in this list focus attention on the need to take precautions against a practice which, some people allege, is undertaken by certain "cowboy" firms in the headhunting market. This is supposed to be a form of industrial espionage in which a non-existent post in a certain area of commerce or industry is advertised by an unscrupulous client for the purpose of squeezing information on competitor firms from unsuspecting candidates. I say "supposed" because I came across not a whisper of this from anyone connected with the recruitment industry. But then an exercise of this kind — if such is ever mounted — would indeed be kept top secret.

In their own hands

With the improbable exception of not being allowed to practise by some extreme Left-wing government of the future, the headhunting industry seems to be faced with considerably fewer problems than most other types of business. As shown in these pages, their acceptability is on the increase, the cost of alternative recruitment methods is rising faster and, come boom or slump, a market is there. The main threat to their future is to be found, in fact, in killing the goose with the golden eggs by pricing their services out of the market; or through disunity bred in neurotic distrust of their competitors. These dangers, I should add, are not so much probable but possible; most of the leading headhunters to whom I talked welcomed the existence of others in the same line of business, as helping to give the fraternity both solidity and respectability.

I shall end with a cautionary tale. Search and selection consultants are of course not infallible, but one of them confirmed their membership of the human race with the story of an assignment to find a marketing director for a firm with a large export business. "We thought we had found the ideal candidate", he said, "the marketing director of a well known U.K. firm. In fact, we were just about to sign the contract in the client's office when the candidate announced that in no circumstances would he consider flying anywhere. Now we had checked his references and he'd been given a full medical, but who'd have thought of asking him a question about that?"

As a rule, I can listen with equanimity to the problems of affluent businessmen who also enjoy their work, but on this occasion, as I sat in his elegant Mayfair office, it was difficult not to feel a certain fleeting sympathy.

The companies and associations referred to and quoted from in this book first appear on the following pages:

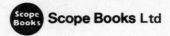

Recent titles also published by

Scope Books Ltd

It CAN be done!

21 studies of small businesses, most of them started from nothing, often in garages or back bedrooms, which have "come good" and now make high profits.

Edited by John M. Ryan   *Publ. 19.4.79*
0 900619 00 9 . . . . Hardback
0 906619 01 7 . . . . Paperback

The Entrepreneurs

A close and careful study of four contemporary businessmen who have built up great empires.

by Elizabeth Hennessy   *Publ. 12.3.80*
0 906619 02 5 . . . . Hardback
0 906619 03 3 . . . . Paperback

How to Manage Your Boss

A penetrating, wickedly accurate observation of how people behave in any management hierarchy, and how to survive in this jungle.

by Raymond Monbiot   *Publ. 23.4.80*
0 906619 04 1 . . . . Hardback
0 906619 05 X . . . . Paperback